CONTENTS

LEON

INTRODUCTION

. . . .

Magic potions. Potions full of love, full of power. Oh, and full of flavour. That is how we see soups at LEON. The stirring of the crucible, the sipping of the broth. What better way to show you love yourself? To show your friends and family that you kinda like them too?

We've had so many kind comments about our Happy Salads *book that we wanted to shine a similar spotlight onto our soups. Some of these we serve in our LEON restaurants, but we just don't have the space on our menu to show off our full repertoire. So, here between these covers, is our best soup work. We've covered our take on classics, and created some new magic recipes (no newts). They are for one or for many. For Monday lunchtime or for a blazing Saturday night.*

Since we started LEON we have been about making it easier for everyone to eat well. We do that by imagining what fast food would be like in heaven and by writing books to share our recipes more widely. Whether you have been eating with us from the beginning or you have just discovered LEON, thank you for being part of the LEON family. We love what we do and we work hard at it. Your support, your ideas, your criticism; it all matters to us and helps us.

Now, go and make some magic.

. . . .

KEY

WF
WHEAT FREE

GF
GLUTEN FREE

DF
DAIRY FREE

V
VEGETARIAN

Ve
VEGAN

PREPPY PREP

CLEANING UP

Wash or peel vegetables before using them in soups, to avoid adding any leftover soil or other nasties to the pan. Rinse herbs and whizz in a salad spinner, or pat dry in a clean tea towel.

TOPPINGS & SWIRLS

A hot soup and a stone-cold topping won't make happy bedfellows. Get the yoghurt, sauce or cheese out of the fridge when you start cooking and allow it to come to room temperature. Don't add crunchy crumbs or croutons until just before you serve, or let guests do it themselves at the table, so they don't have a chance to sink or go soggy.

BLENDING

Jug blenders give smoother results more quickly than stick blenders, but stick blenders will do the job if you take your time. Both require a bit of care – stick blenders can cause hot splurts and splashes, especially if the soup is shallow in your pan. Jug blenders should never be filled to the top with hot soup – this will cause a vacuum and they can explode. Find out the maximum fill point from the manufacturer and never go over it.

(Rebecca also discovered that, unlike food processors, blenders will happily run without a lid on if you leave the ON button pressed . . . Nowadays, lesson learned and butternut squash washed out of her hair, she takes the jug off, fills it over the pan and makes sure the lid is on before starting the motor.)

STOCKY STOCK

THE IMPORTANCE OF GOOD STOCK

Is there anything more homely than a pan of chicken stock bubbling away the evening after a Sunday roast? We love making our own stock – we know exactly what's gone into it, we can tailor it to our favourite flavours and it lasts almost forever in the freezer (especially as ice cubes). Here are our top tips for perfect stock. (For stock recipes, see pages 214–18.)

If you're making your own stock, don't add salt. This allows you to control how much you add to a dish when you come to cook later. (Technically, only broth should be seasoned.)

Add herbs that complement whatever you plan to use the stock for, but be sparing – you don't want a rosemary or thyme infusion. When cooking, keep stock at a low simmer and skim off the fat, rather than letting it boil hard. A fast boil will cause the fat to emulsify into the water and make the stock cloudy.

Of course, sometimes, there just isn't time to make stock from scratch. But some powdered and cubed stocks or bouillons contain a lot of salt, so if you're using these, choose a good-quality, low-salt, no-salt or low-sodium product, partly for health and partly so you can choose how much to season your soup.

If you want to use cubes or powder, then, unless you're vegetarian, good-quality chicken stock cubes often give nicer results than vegetable stock cubes, which can be a bit too powerful. Vegetarians and vegans can make their soups with weak stock to avoid this problem. We reckon it's almost always best to make or buy fresh fish stock rather than using a fishy stock cube. If that's impossible, use chicken or vegetable stock instead.

Sometimes, the delicate flavour of a particular soup might be ruined by a stock cube or powder – we've said so in the recipe where that is the case.

Whichever type you use, make sure your stock is piping hot before you start cooking.

SOUPER STORECUPBOARD

TINS, JARS & BOTTLES

Fish sauce

Chilli oil

Coconut milk

Miso paste

Tomatoes

Soy sauce

Olive oil for cooking

Extra virgin olive oil

DRIED

Noodles

Small pasta

Seaweed

Rice

Barley

VEGETABLES & FRUIT

Onions & shallots

Celery

Carrots

Garlic

Potatoes

Spring onions

Limes

Lemons

Lemongrass

Ginger

Chillies

Leeks

Lime leaves

Galangal

Fresh bay leaves

Peppers

FREEZER

Sweetcorn

Cooking chorizo

Broad beans

Pancetta or bacon

Homemade stock

Peas

NUTS & SEEDS

Pumpkin

Linseeds

Almonds

Sesame

Pine nuts

Pistachios

Hazelnuts

SPICES

Curry leaves

Mustard seeds

Cumin

Coriander

Smoked & sweet paprika

Black pepper

Cayenne pepper

Nutmeg

Fennel seeds

Caraway seeds

Chilli flakes

Dried chillies

Garam masala

Cardamom

Turmeric

FRIDGE

Parmesan

Yoghurt

Tofu

Halloumi

Feta

Fresh herbs

Soured cream

Crème fraiche

Cream

PULSES

Chickpeas

White beans

Split red lentils

Green lentils

Urid (black) dal

Split peas

Gram flour

Puy lentils

Black beans

NATURALLY FAST

CARROT, CUMIN & CORIANDER

SERVES 4

PREP TIME: 10 MINS • COOK TIME: 30 MINS

WF • GF • V (if made with vegetable stock) • (DF • Ve if labneh is omitted)

1 tablespoon **olive oil**

1 **onion**, chopped

450g **carrots**, chopped

½ teaspoon **coriander seeds**

½ teaspoon **cumin seeds**

1 litre hot **chicken** or **vegetable stock**

a handful of **fresh coriander leaves**

TO SERVE:

4 tablespoons **labneh** (see page 183)

dukkah (see page 190)

flatbreads (see page 210)

Our version of a classic soup, and perfect for getting through a glut of carrots.

Place a large saucepan with a lid over a fairly low heat and add the oil. When hot, add the onion and carrots and cook gently, stirring often, for 15 minutes.

Meanwhile, toast the spices in a hot dry pan for a minute or two, just until fragrant – they can scorch quickly, so keep watch. Tip into a pestle and mortar and grind to a powder.

Add the ground spices to the pan of carrots, then pour in the hot stock. Bring to a simmer and cook for about 15 minutes, or until the carrots are really tender. Remove from the heat, add the coriander leaves and blend until smooth.

Add a dollop of labneh and a sprinkling of dukkah to each bowl and serve with flatbreads on the side.

\\\\ TIP ////

Top with flaked almonds, toasted for a few minutes in a dry pan until golden.

SMOKED HADDOCK CHOWDER

SERVES 2

PREP TIME: 10 MINS • COOK TIME: 30 MINS

WF • GF (but check chorizo)

500ml **whole milk**

250g **undyed smoked haddock fillets**, or any **smoked white fish**

a knob of **butter**

½ an **onion**, finely sliced into half moons

1 **leek**, finely sliced

350g **potatoes**, about 3½ medium potatoes, peeled and cut into 1-cm cubes

pinch of **lemon zest**

salt and **freshly ground black** (or **white**) **pepper**

TO SERVE:

a handful of **frazzled chorizo** (see page 192)

1 tablespoon **finely chopped fresh chives**

A September fishing trip, a walk along the dock, a drink on the pier, a soup.

Pour the milk into a large saucepan. Bring to a simmer over a medium heat, then slide in the fish. Bring back to a simmer, then cook for 2 minutes. Lift the fish from the milk, setting the milk aside, and leave to cool a little.

Meanwhile, place a frying pan over a low heat and add the butter. When melted, add the onion, leek and a pinch of salt, and cook without colouring until just soft and translucent, about 8–10 minutes.

When the fish is cool enough to handle, flake it into bite-sized pieces, removing any skin or bones as you go. Set aside.

Return the pan of milk to the heat and add the cooked onion and leek along with the potatoes. Bring to a simmer and cook until the potatoes are tender, about 10–15 minutes.

Return the fish to the pan and warm through for a minute or two. Add the lemon zest, season with black pepper and add a little more salt if necessary – smoked fish can vary a lot in its salt content.

Serve with the frazzled chorizo and chopped chives sprinkled over the top of the soup.

TIP

Try adding sweetcorn, chopped, cooked and squeezed-out spinach, or a poached egg to each serving.

A-MAIZING CHOWDER

SERVES 4
PREP TIME: 10 MINS • COOK TIME: 25 MINS
V (if made with vegetable stock)

. . . .

4 cobs of **fresh corn**, or
   300g **frozen sweetcorn**

125g **floury potatoes**, about 1 medium
   potato, peeled and diced

500ml hot **chicken** or **vegetable stock**

a knob of **butter**

½ an **onion**, finely chopped

1 stick of **celery**, finely chopped

2 cloves of **garlic**, finely chopped

1 tablespoon **flour**

350ml **milk**

salt and **freshly ground black pepper**

spring onions, or **fresh chives**, sliced,
   to garnish

A fresh-tasting, slightly sweet soup, and a great supper for kids.

. . . .

Stand each cob on its end and use a sharp knife to strip the corn from the cob. Put the corn kernels, the naked cobs and the potatoes into a large pan and add the hot stock. Bring to the boil and cook for 15 minutes, or until the potato is soft and the kernels are tender. Remove and discard the naked cobs. If you are using frozen sweetcorn it won't need so long to cook, just add it to the pan when the potato is soft and simmer for 3–4 minutes.

Meanwhile, place a frying pan on a medium heat and add the butter. Once foaming add the onion, celery and a pinch of salt, and cook gently, stirring often, until the onion is translucent, about 8 minutes. Add the garlic and the flour and cook for another minute, then remove from the heat.

Add the contents of the frying pan and the milk to the saucepan with the potatoes and sweetcorn. Stir well and bring to a simmer. Remove from the heat and blend some or all of the soup until smooth, depending on the texture you prefer. Taste for seasoning and add more salt and pepper if necessary.

Serve garnished with the spring onions or chives.

> ### \\\\ TIP ////
> Adding a tablespoon of spicy chipotle paste or a handful of smoked diced bacon takes this soup to another level. Alternatively, melt a tablespoon of butter per person, remove from the heat and add a teaspoon of hot or sweet smoked paprika to the butter, mix, then swirl through the soup.

KERALAN-STYLE SEAFOOD

SERVES 4

PREP TIME: 10 MINS · COOK TIME: 30 MINS

WF · GF · DF

700g **fish fillets** – **hake**, **salmon**, **cod**, **haddock** or a mixture, cut into chunks

2 teaspoons **ground turmeric**

2 tablespoons **vegetable oil**

1½ teaspoons **mustard seeds**

4 **shallots**, finely sliced

10 **curry leaves**

2 cloves of **garlic**, crushed to a paste

4-cm piece of **fresh ginger**, peeled and finely grated

1 medium **green chilli**, seeded and finely sliced

2 medium **tomatoes**, halved, cored, seeded and sliced

2 × 400ml tins of **full-fat coconut milk**

1–2 teaspoons **fresh lime juice**

salt and **freshly ground black pepper**

TO SERVE:

fresh coriander leaves

steamed rice

This is inspired by meen moilee, a Keralan fish curry. Briefly frying the fish gives it a more inviting texture than simply poaching it. Use full-fat coconut milk – lower-fat coconut milk often curdles when cooked.

Pat the fish fillets dry, then season with 1 teaspoon of the turmeric and a good dusting of salt and pepper. Toss to ensure each piece is lightly covered.

Pour the oil into a large heavy-based saucepan with a lid set over a high heat. Add the seasoned fish pieces and fry for a minute or two, turning once. Before they are fully cooked, gently remove from the pan and set aside.

Lower the heat to medium. Add the mustard seeds and when they start to crackle, add the shallots, curry leaves and remaining turmeric. Cook, stirring, until the shallot begins to brown, about 5 minutes. Next, add the garlic, ginger, chilli and tomatoes and cook, stirring, for a minute. Add 3 tablespoons of water and cook until the tomatoes are just beginning to soften – stirring gently so as not to pulverize the tomato. Turn the heat right down and add the coconut milk. Very slowly, bring it to simmering point – boiling coconut milk too quickly will make it split.

Once simmering, return the fish pieces to the pan, submerging them in the broth, and put the lid on. Cook for 3 minutes, or until the fish is just cooked. Remove from the heat, add 1 teaspoon of the lime juice and then taste, adding more salt, pepper or the rest of the lime juice, as necessary.

Serve garnished with coriander leaves and with some steamed rice on the side.

\\\\| TIP |///

Vegetarians and vegans can make this with sweet potato instead of fish, cooked until nearly done in salted water, then finished in the broth. Or try wilted greens and cooked chickpeas, or green beans, cooked for a few minutes in the soup before serving.

REBECCA'S STRACCIATELLA

SERVES 6

PREP TIME: 5 MINS • COOK TIME: 12 MINS

2 litres good-quality **chicken stock**

200g of the smallest **pasta** you can find,
   like **stelline** or **tuffoli**

2 **eggs**

sea salt and **freshly ground black
   pepper**

TO SERVE:

a handful of **fresh parsley**, chopped

freshly grated **Parmesan**, to serve

*The brilliant Rebecca Di Mambro is in charge of innovation at LEON.
She reckons this is one of the easiest soups to make, and one of the
tastiest. It's a traditional Italian soup, normally served at the beginning
of a big feast such as Easter lunch. Or, in Rebecca's family, by her Uncle
John and his husband Alan as the starter course of Christmas dinner.*

Bring the chicken stock to the boil and add the pasta. Cooking time will be around
8–10 minutes, depending on the pasta.

Crack the eggs into a small bowl and beat to combine, then season with the salt
and pepper.

When the pasta is ready, turn down the heat to a simmer and slowly pour in the egg.

Wait for around 30 seconds for the egg to cook in the hot stock, then whisk
vigorously to break the egg up into 'little strands' (the rough English translation of
the Italian name).

Serve immediately, garnishing with the fresh parsley and a generous sprinkling of
the Parmesan.

\ \ \ | TIP | / / /
Stir an extra handful of freshly
grated Parmesan into the beaten
egg mix. A squeeze of lemon would
also be a great finish to this.

TOM YUM (YUM YUM)

SERVES 4 as a starter, or 2 as a main course
PREP TIME: 15 MINS • COOK TIME: 12 MINS
GF · DF

- -

200g sustainably sourced **raw prawns**

1 litre **boiling water**

1 stick of **lemongrass**, lightly bruised

3-cm piece of **galangal**, roughly sliced

6 **lime leaves**, torn into pieces

1 **hot red chilli** and 1 **mild green chilli**,
  sliced into rings (seed the red chilli and
  use just half if you don't like heat)

6 cloves of **garlic**, peeled

1 teaspoon **palm** or **brown sugar**

50g **oyster mushrooms**, torn into
  bite-sized pieces

1 tablespoon **fish sauce**, or more, to taste

juice of 1 **lime**, or more, to taste

coriander, sliced, to serve

This is an invigorating, spicy Thai soup made with prawns and oyster mushrooms, flavoured with chilli, lemongrass, galangal and lime leaves. It will clear your head (and your sinuses). Galangal is now commonly available in large supermarkets – look for it alongside the fresh herbs and chillies.

The cooking process is very quick, so have everything ready to go before you start. Don't be surprised that this version of tom yum is pale, not red – the colour comes from using Thai roasted chilli paste, nam phrik phao (see tip below), or ready-made tom yum paste.

- -

Peel and de-vein the prawns, if necessary. (Do this by running a sharp knife along the back of the prawn, then use its tip to pull out the black thread running the length of the prawn. Discard.) Set aside.

Pour the boiling water into a saucepan set over a medium heat. Add the bruised lemongrass, galangal, lime leaves, chilli and garlic, and simmer together for about 8 minutes. Bring up to a steady boil, then add the sugar, mushrooms and prawns. Cover with a lid and cook for 3 minutes, or until the prawns are pink and cooked through.

Remove from the heat and add the fish sauce and lime juice, then taste and decide if you would like to add more of either.

Ladle the soup into large bowls, leaving behind the lemongrass stalk and as much of the lime leaves, garlic and galangal as you can, as none of these are good to eat. Garnish with the coriander and eat straight away.

\\\ TIP ///

Try this with chicken or chunks of firm-fleshed fish, or make it vegetarian by poaching Asian greens, broccoli, beans and pepper in the broth. For the classic red colour, swirl in a spoonful of Thai roasted chilli paste, *nam phrik phao*, at the end of cooking.

SUPER SOUP

SERVES 4
PREP TIME: 10 MINS • COOK TIME: 12 MINS
WF • GF • V • Ve (if feta is omitted)

2 tablespoons **olive oil**

3 **spring onions**, trimmed and
   finely chopped

100g **cucumber** (about 8cm of a
   cucumber), seeds scooped out and
   discarded, flesh chopped

800ml hot **vegetable stock**

300g **broccoli**, about 1 head, sliced
   into florets

350g **frozen peas**

1 tablespoon **chopped fresh parsley**, plus
   extra to serve

1 tablespoon **chopped fresh mint**, plus
   extra to serve

2 teaspoons **lemon juice**

salt and freshly ground black pepper

TO SERVE:
about 150g **feta**, crumbled
puffed and popped seeds (see page 191)

*This is inspired by our best-selling super salad, but without the quinoa.
We think quinoa is a bit weird in soup.*

*Cooked cucumber isn't as strange as it sounds — try it gently and briefly
sautéd in butter and served with grilled fish, and you'll be a convert.*

Pour the oil into a large heavy-based pan with a lid and set it over a low heat. Add the
spring onions and a pinch of salt and cook for 5 minutes; don't allow to brown. Add
the chopped cucumber and cook for a couple of minutes, stirring. Add the stock,
broccoli and peas and bring to the boil. Simmer for 3–4 minutes. Add the herbs,
some pepper and the lemon juice, remove from the heat, then blend the soup until
smooth. Taste and add a little more seasoning if necessary.

Serve with the crumbled feta, a little more mint and parsley, and the puffed and
popped seeds.

TIP
If using fresh peas, they
need slightly longer in the
pot, so add them 5 minutes
before the broccoli.

COOL BEANS

SERVES 4 as a starter, or 2 as a main course
PREP TIME: 20 MINS • COOK TIME: 30 MINS
WF • GF • V (if made with vegetable stock)

a knob of **butter** or 1 tablespoon **olive oil**

1 **onion**, diced

2 cloves of **garlic**, crushed

6 **parsley stalks**, finely chopped

1 sprig of **fresh thyme**

2 tablespoons **rice**

500ml hot **chicken** or **vegetable stock**

500g **broad beans**, fresh or frozen,
   podded, reserving a handful to serve

4 tablespoons **Greek yoghurt**

1 teaspoon **lemon juice**

salt and **freshly ground black pepper**

TO SERVE:

garlic yoghurt (see page 170), at room
   temperature

2 teaspoons **chopped fresh dill**

To make this dairy-free and vegan, use oil instead of butter and omit the yoghurt added at the end. The rice gives the soup a velvety texture, but doesn't add any flavour.

Put the butter or oil into a large heavy-based pan with a lid over a medium heat, add the onion and a pinch of salt, cook for 8 minutes, then add the garlic, parsley and thyme. Add the rice to the pan, stir a couple of times, then add the hot stock. Simmer for 20 minutes until the rice is really soft. Add the broad beans and bring back to a simmer, just enough to heat through. Remove from the heat, fish out the thyme, and blend the soup until smooth.

Pour back into the pan but don't return to the heat. Put the yoghurt into a bowl and add a couple of tablespoons of the hot soup, whisk smooth, then add another 2 tablespoons and whisk again, to temper the yoghurt.

Pour this mixture into the soup pan and whisk until smooth. Add the lemon juice, then taste and add some freshly ground pepper, plus more salt, if necessary.

Serve with a dollop of garlic yoghurt swirled through the soup and topped with the chopped fresh dill and a few of the reserved shelled broad beans.

\\\ TIP ///

Just like peas, broad beans are natural partners for both smoky pork and mint – try swapping the dill for chopped fresh mint, or add finely chopped rashers of bacon along with the onion. You can substitute up to half the beans with peas, if you like.

KOREAN-STYLE KIMCHI SOUP

SERVES 2

PREP TIME: 10 MINS • COOK TIME: 12 MINS

WF • GF • DF

. . . .

1 tablespoon **sesame** or **vegetable oil**

½ an **onion**, finely chopped

1 teaspoon **Korean sriracha chilli sauce** (or more if you love heat)

½ a **courgette**, cut into 1-cm chunks

2 dried or preserved **anchovies** or 3 dashes of **Worcestershire sauce**

100g **kimchi**, drained and finely chopped, plus 3 tablespoons juice from the jar

75g **mushrooms**, sliced

1 teaspoon **soy sauce**

2 cloves of **garlic**, crushed

600ml hot **chicken** or **vegetable stock**

200g **silken tofu**

2 **eggs** (optional)

spring onions, finely chopped, to garnish

Kimchi is a fermented chilli and cabbage condiment from Korea, which is now easy to find in supermarkets and online. This tangy, spicy soup is inspired by a Korean dish called **soondubu jjigae.** *It's easy to make and packs a major punch – plus it's really healthy. Serve with some steamed rice.*

. . . .

Set a wide, deep pan over a medium-high heat. Add the oil, onion, sriracha, courgette, anchovies or Worcestershire sauce, drained kimchi, mushrooms and soy sauce. Cook, stirring occasionally, for 5 minutes. Add the garlic and cook for 1 minute, then add the stock and kimchi juice, and bring to the boil.

Silken tofu is quite fragile, so open the packet carefully. Use a knife or spoon to break it into large chunks, then slide them into the simmering broth. Don't stir vigorously or it will fall apart.

Cook for 3 minutes. Taste the broth and decide if you would like more spicy sriracha. Turn the heat right down and crack in the eggs, if using. Allow the eggs to poach in the broth to your liking (about 2 minutes is our preference) and serve straight away, carefully ladling the eggs and tofu into bowls. Garnish with the spring onions.

> ＼＼＼ **TIP** ／／／
>
> Turn this into a vegetarian or vegan dish by omitting the anchovies or Worcestershire sauce, and the eggs. For meat lovers, you can add thin strips of pork belly or steak to the broth before the tofu; simmer for about 15 minutes.

BROCCOLI & BLUE CHEESE

SERVES 4

PREP TIME: 5 MINS • COOK TIME: 35 MINS

WF • GF • V (if made with vegetable stock)

2 tablespoons **butter** or **olive oil**

2 **onions**, diced

200g **potatoes**, about 2 medium
   potatoes, peeled and diced

1 litre hot **chicken** or **vegetable stock**

2 heads of **broccoli**, about 500g,
   roughly chopped

1½ teaspoons **lemon juice**

75g–150g **blue cheese**, crumbled into
   small pieces, plus extra to serve

a pinch of freshly grated **nutmeg**

3 tablespoons **single** or **double cream**
   (optional), plus extra to serve

salt and **freshly ground black pepper**

6 tablespoons **flaked almonds**, to serve

A healthily indulgent combination of super vegetables and rich cheese. A quiche in a bowl. In a good way.

Place a large pan over a low heat. Add the butter or oil, diced onions and a pinch of salt and cook gently until the onion is soft, about 10 minutes. Add the diced potatoes and hot stock and simmer until the potatoes are tender, about 12 minutes.

Meanwhile, toast the almonds in a hot dry pan for 2 or 3 minutes, until golden – keep watch, as they can burn easily. Set aside until ready to serve.

Add the broccoli and lemon juice to the soup and simmer for 5 minutes, or until the broccoli is just tender. Use a blender to process the soup until completely smooth. Return to the pan, but keep off the heat. Crumble in 75g of the cheese, and stir until it has completely melted. Taste and decide how much more you would like to add – it really depends on how pungent your cheese is.

Season with the nutmeg and some black pepper. Stir in the cream, if using, and serve scattered with the toasted flaked almonds, a little crumbled cheese and a drizzle of cream.

\\\\ TIP ////

If reheating this soup, don't boil it once the cheese is incorporated, as the cheese will split and become lumpy.

MOHINGA

SERVES 2

PREP TIME: 15 MINS • COOK TIME: 35 MINS

WF • GF • DF

3-cm piece of **fresh ginger**, peeled

2 cloves of **garlic**

1 stick of **lemongrass**

⅛ teaspoon **chilli powder**

1 teaspoon **ground turmeric**

1 tablespoon **flavourless oil**, plus extra
     if needed

3 **shallots**, finely sliced

2 tablespoons **rice flour**

2 tablespoons **gram flour**

1 litre hot **fish stock** (not from a cube, see
     page 216)

2 teaspoons **fish sauce**

350g **white fish (cod, bream** or **haddock)**,
     chopped into chunks

100g cooked **rice vermicelli noodles**

salt

**ANY OR ALL OF THE FOLLOWING,
TO SERVE:**

crispy onions (see page 193)

2 **marinated eggs** (see page 66)

fresh coriander leaves, roughly chopped

lime wedges

2 **spring onions**, finely chopped

1 teaspoon **finely chopped red chilli**

Mohinga is a Burmese fish soup, often made at the roadside and eaten for breakfast. It's made with river catfish, but you can use any firm white fish if you can't get your hands on catfish.

Start by preparing the crispy onions and marinated eggs (see pages 193 and 66) to serve, if using.

Blitz together the ginger, garlic, lemongrass, chilli powder, turmeric and oil until you get a rough purée. Set a large pan over a low heat, and add the paste once it is hot. Fry gently for a couple of minutes, then add the shallots and a pinch of salt, with a little more oil if the pan looks dry or if the paste is sticking. Cook for 10 minutes to soften the shallots without browning, stirring often.

Toast the rice flour and gram flour separately in a dry pan set over a medium heat, until pale brown, which will take just a minute or two. Whisk the toasted flours into the stock until smooth, then add to the onion and spice mixture with the fish sauce. Simmer for 10 minutes, stirring occasionally and scraping the bottom so nothing sticks, until thickened.

Finally, add the fish and the cooked noodles. Simmer for 3 minutes. Serve in deep, wide bowls, with your choice of coriander leaves, lime wedges, crispy onions, chopped spring onion, chilli and egg.

ROASTED RED PEPPER

SERVES 4

PREP TIME: 10 MINS • COOK TIME: 35 MINS

WF • GF • DF • (V • Ve if made with vegetable stock)

5 **red peppers**

3 tablespoons **olive oil**

2 **onions**, diced

2 **carrots**, diced

2 sticks of **celery**, diced

1 clove of **garlic**, finely chopped

1 teaspoon **tomato purée**

1 teaspoon **smoked paprika**

800ml hot **chicken** or **vegetable stock**

salt and **freshly ground black pepper**

TO SERVE:

extra virgin olive oil

gremolata (see page 179)

You can cheat and use peppers from a jar, but you won't get the same deliciously smoky flavour you get from flame-cooking them yourself. A fistful of frazzled chorizo (see page 192) thrown on top at the end is delicious here.

Hold the whole red peppers directly over a gas ring and cook, turning, until blistered and blackened all over. Alternatively, heat the grill to its highest setting, halve the peppers and grill, skin side up, until blackened in the same way.

When done, seal the peppers into plastic sandwich bags and leave to steam and cool.

Meanwhile, place a large saucepan over a medium heat. Add the oil, onions, carrots, celery, a pinch of salt and pepper and cook, stirring often, for 10 minutes. Then add the garlic and tomato purée and cook for a couple of minutes, stirring again. Add the smoked paprika and the stock, and bring to a simmer. Simmer for 10 minutes, or until the vegetables are tender.

The peppers should now be cool enough to handle. Rub off the blackened skins and discard, then remove the stalks, seeds and ribs. (Don't rinse them, as you'll lose the flavour.) Chop into bite-sized pieces and add to the pan of stock, then simmer for a further 5 minutes. Remove from the heat and blend until completely smooth. Taste and add more seasoning, if necessary. Reduce a little on the hob if you feel the soup isn't quite thick enough — peppers can release a lot of liquid.

Serve with a drizzle of extra virgin olive oil and a sprinkling of gremolata.

\\\\ TIP ////

For creamy soup, add a spoonful of — surprise! — cream or soured cream per bowl. For a Mexican-style twist, omit the garnish above and finish with chopped avocado, feta, coriander, fresh lime and chilli, or a dollop of guacamole (see page 178).

AJO BLANCO

SERVES 4 as a small starter

PREP TIME: 5–15 MINS • CHILL TIME: at least 2 HOURS

DF • V • Ve

1 slice of **slightly stale white bread**, crusts removed

100g **blanched almonds**

2 cloves of **garlic**, crushed to a paste

100ml **extra virgin olive oil**

1 tablespoon **sherry vinegar**

250–300ml **ice-cold water**

salt

TO SERVE:

extra virgin olive oil

4 **white grapes**, halved

4 **apple slices**

4 **cucumber slices**, halved

freshly ground black pepper

For really authentic ajo blanco, a chilled almond and garlic soup from Spain, you should blanch the almonds yourself. It's quite a fiddly job, though (soak unblanched almonds in boiling water for 5 minutes, then remove the skins), so using blanched almonds is fine by us. It's both very rich and very garlicky, so serve it in small quantities.

Rip the bread into small pieces. Place in a bowl and cover with a couple of tablespoons of water; leave to soak for 5 minutes.

Put the soaked bread, blanched almonds, garlic paste, oil, vinegar and a pinch of salt into a blender, along with 100ml of the ice-cold water. Process until completely smooth, scooping any unblended almonds up from beneath the blades with a spatula. Add more water as necessary until the soup has a rich pouring consistency, about that of whipping cream. Chill for at least 2 hours before serving. Taste and add more salt or vinegar, if necessary, after chilling.

Divide between 4 small bowls and serve with a little extra virgin olive oil, the grapes, apple and cucumber, and a little black pepper.

COURGETTE & GREEN HERB

SERVES 2
PREP TIME: 5 MINS • COOK TIME: 25 MINS
WF • GF

2 tablespoons **olive oil**

500g **courgettes**, roughly chopped

2 cloves of **garlic**, quartered

450ml hot **chicken** or **vegetable stock**

1 tablespoon **very finely chopped fresh parsley**

1 tablespoon **very finely chopped fresh basil**

a pinch of **freshly grated nutmeg**, plus extra to serve

salt and **freshly ground black pepper**

TO SERVE:

grated **Parmesan**

3 tablespoons **double cream**

This soup is beautifully summery, and can even be served chilled on a hot sunny day.

Place a large pan over a very low heat. Add the oil, then the courgettes, garlic and a pinch of salt. Cook the vegetables very gently, stirring often, for 20–25 minutes, until the courgettes are really soft and the garlic is just browning.

Add the stock, turn up the heat and simmer for 2 minutes. Remove from the heat, add the chopped herbs, and blend the soup until smooth and bright green.

Stir through the nutmeg, plus some salt and pepper, as necessary. Serve each portion with a generous dusting of Parmesan, a drizzle of cream and an extra sprinkling of nutmeg.

\\\ TIP ///
You can swap the basil and parsley for the leaves from a sprig of mint.

PUY LENTILS, BACON & MUSTARD CREAM

SERVES 2

PREP TIME: 10 MINS · COOK TIME: 40 MINS

WF · GF

1 tablespoon **flavourless oil**

a knob of **butter**

2 rashers of **smoked streaky bacon**, very finely diced

2 **shallots**, very finely diced

2 cloves of **garlic**, crushed

150g **Puy lentils**, rinsed

750ml **hot water**

2 whole sprigs of **fresh parsley**

1 **bay leaf**

100g **chard**, leaves only (2–3 large leaves), finely shredded

4 tablespoons **single cream**, at room temperature

2 teaspoons **smooth Dijon mustard**

2 teaspoons **lemon juice**

salt and **freshly ground black pepper**

TO SERVE:

fresh parsley leaves, chopped

spring onion or **chives**, chopped

This is a spin on the classic French Puy lentil salad, warmed up and turned into a rich soup with a mustardy topping.

Place the oil in a large heavy-based saucepan with a lid, set over a medium heat. Add the butter and, when hot, add the bacon and cook until just beginning to crisp up. Add the shallots and cook, stirring for about 7 minutes, until translucent, but not browning. Next, add the garlic and cook for 1 minute.

Add the Puy lentils, water, parsley and bay leaf to the pan and bring to a simmer. Cover and cook for 20–25 minutes, or until the lentils are tender (unlike other lentils, Puy don't go soft and mushy, and will keep their shape during cooking). Add a pinch of salt and some freshly ground black pepper, plus the chard, and cook until the chard has just wilted.

Meanwhile, whisk together the cream and mustard.

Remove the lentil pan from the heat and stir in the lemon juice, then remove the bay leaf and parsley sprigs and discard. Taste and add more seasoning, if necessary. Serve the soup topped with a spoonful or two of the mustard cream, the chopped parsley and the spring onion or chives.

YOU MAKE MISO HAPPY

SERVES 4

PREP TIME: 10 MINS • COOK TIME: 5 MINS

WF • GF • DF • (V • Ve if made with kombu or vegetable stock)

150g **firm silken tofu**

a handful of **dried wakame
seaweed**, shredded

1 litre hot **dashi broth**, **kombu broth** or
vegetable stock

4 tablespoons **miso paste**

150g **pak choi** or other **Asian
greens**, chopped

2 **spring onions**, very finely chopped

*Miso soup is made with dashi broth, which gets its umami-rich flavour
from simmering a mixture of seaweed, mushrooms and dried bonito fish.
If making this for vegetarians, you should omit the dashi and use either
good-quality vegetable stock or kombu broth, which is made without fish.
Both miso paste and dashi in sachets or powder are easy to find online
and in some large supermarkets.*

Open the tofu packet carefully, so as not to damage or crumble the tofu, then cut into 1-cm dice.

Place the wakame seaweed in a bowl of hot water and leave to rehydrate.

Put the broth or stock into a saucepan and set over a low heat. Blend the miso paste with a couple of tablespoons of hot stock, then whisk it into the rest of the stock. Add the tofu and the greens and cook for 1 minute.

Remove from the heat and divide between 4 bowls. Finish by draining the seaweed and dividing it and the chopped spring onions between the portions.

\\\\ TIP ////

Serve with a little homemade
pickled ginger on the side (see
page 194). Make this light soup
more substantial by adding
some grilled fish, sautéd
mushrooms or noodles. Miso
settles, so give it a good swish
before taking each spoonful.

COMFORTING

OODLES OF NOODLES

SERVES 4

PREP TIME: 10 MINS • COOK TIME: 1 HOUR 10 MINS

DF

. . . .

1 **chicken**, approx 1.5kg

2 **carrots**, peeled and roughly chopped

2 **leeks**, outer leaves and green top
   discarded, roughly chopped

1 stick of **celery**, roughly chopped

½ an **onion**, roughly chopped

1 clove of **garlic**, whole but bashed with
   the flat of a knife

10 **black peppercorns**

225g **spaghetti**, **tagliatelle** or **linguine**,
   broken into short lengths, or other
   short pasta

salt and **freshly ground black pepper**

A soothing soup for cold winter days, this has become a staple on the LEON menu. Rebecca's dad also made a simple version of this chicken soup at weekends when she was little, so that's the way she likes it now, but here we've added some finely diced carrot and finely chopped fresh leek towards the end of cooking (the vegetables used to make the broth will be too squishy, so these should be discarded). For fun, go check out the heated debate online about whether it has medicinal properties. Where do you stand?

. . . .

Place a pan with a lid, one big enough to hold the chicken and all the vegetables, over a medium heat. Place the whole chicken in the pan, then tuck half the carrot and leek, the celery, onion and garlic around it. Pour over enough boiling water to cover the chicken, then add the peppercorns and a good pinch of salt. Bring back to the boil, then turn down to a simmer and cover.

Poach the chicken for about an hour. (If any part of the chicken is poking out of the liquid, turn it over, using tongs, halfway through cooking.) Remove from the heat and let the chicken cool in the broth. When cool enough to handle, lift the chicken out of the broth, let it drain and then place on a board. Pull the meat from the bones and discard the skin and bones. Shred the meat into bite-sized pieces. Set aside.

Skim off any scum which has formed on the broth, and any fat which has collected on the surface, then strain the broth into a bowl, discarding all the now-mushy vegetables. Pour the broth back into the pan and add the chicken. Taste for seasoning — you will probably want to add another generous pinch of salt and lots of freshly ground black pepper.

Return the pan to the heat, bring to a simmer and add the broken spaghetti. Cook for 7 minutes, or until al dente, adding the new carrot and leek halfway through. Serve straight away.

\\\\ TIP ////

Throw in a handful of frozen sweetcorn for the last 5 minutes of cooking, or some chopped mushrooms which have been sautéed gently in butter. For a gluten-free version, try rice noodles.

WINTER MINESTRONE

SERVES 4

PREP TIME: 10 MINS • COOK TIME: 50 MINS

DF (if cheese is omitted)

· ·

1 tablespoon **olive oil**

1 **onion**, finely diced

1 **leek**, trimmed and finely chopped

1 **carrot**, finely diced

1 stick of **celery**, finely diced

75g **smoked bacon**, about 2 rashers, or
  pancetta (optional), rind removed,
  very finely chopped

1 clove of **garlic**, crushed

2 teaspoons **tomato purée**

200g **tinned chopped tomatoes**

750ml hot **chicken** or **vegetable stock**

a small pinch of **fresh thyme leaves**

1 **bay leaf**

400g tin of **cannellini beans**, drained

85g **small pasta**, like **macaroni**, broken
  spaghetti or small **pasta shells**

100g **kale** or **Savoy cabbage**, ribs
  removed, leaves shredded

salt and **freshly ground black pepper**

grated **Parmesan**, to serve

There are dozens of recipes for minestrone, which means 'big soup' ('maxistrone') in Italian. It can be made at any time of year, using whatever seasonal vegetables you have, and the only rule – if there can be said to be any at all – is that you also include some little hunks of starch in it. These could be pasta, potatoes or pulses, or a combination. (See also the spring minestrone with pesto on page 112.)

The habit of adding tinned tomatoes is a British invention, rather than Italian, but one which Rebecca loves, having grown up with it. The bacon or pancetta is not essential, but if you use any be sure to cut it up into tiny pieces, as otherwise you will be left with slightly rubbery, not totally appetizing strips of boiled meat, when all you really want is a subtle hint of porkiness in the broth.

· ·

Place a large saucepan with a lid over a medium heat. Add the oil and when hot add the onion, leek, carrot, celery and salt and cook, stirring often, for about 10 minutes. The aim is to let the vegetables sweat rather than colour, so turn the heat down if you see them beginning to brown. Next, add the bacon, if using, garlic and tomato purée, and cook for another 5 minutes, again stirring often.

Pour in the tomatoes and cook for a minute or so, then add the hot stock, thyme and bay leaf. Bring to a simmer, then cover and leave for about 20 minutes.

Add the beans, pasta and kale or cabbage and cook for 1 minute less than the pasta packet instructions suggest, or until the pasta is al dente. Taste and adjust the seasoning if necessary. If the soup seems closer to a stew than a soup, add a little boiling water to loosen it – pasta can absorb a lot of liquid as it cooks.

Serve in wide bowls, with plenty of freshly grated Parmesan.

\\\ TIP ///

Rebecca once worked on a video shoot with Gordon Ramsay (clang!) – instead of Parmesan, he topped his minestrone with feta: scrumptious.

LEEK & POTATO SOUP

SERVES 4

PREP TIME: 10 MINS • COOK TIME: 25 MINS

WF · GF · V (if made with vegetable stock)

1 tablespoon **olive oil**, or a knob of **butter**

2 **onions**, diced

4 **leeks**, trimmed and sliced

4 sprigs of **fresh thyme**

500g **floury white potatoes**, about
    4 medium potatoes, peeled and diced

1 litre hot **chicken** or **vegetable stock**

250ml **whole milk**

125ml **single cream**

salt and **freshly ground black pepper**

chopped fresh chives, to serve

Made by Marion. A simple, warming and classic soup and a speciality of John's mum.

Place a large heavy-based pan with a lid over a medium heat. Add the oil or butter and then the onions, leeks, a pinch of salt and pepper. Sweat the vegetables gently for 10 minutes, stirring often. Next, add the thyme, potatoes and stock. Bring to a simmer, cover, and cook until the potatoes are tender, 10–15 minutes.

Add the milk, bring back to a simmer, then remove from the heat. Remove the thyme. Blend some or all of the soup until very smooth, depending on your preferred texture. Stir in the cream. Taste and add more seasoning, if necessary. Serve garnished with the chives.

\\\\ **TIP** ////
Add some frazzled pancetta (see page 192), grated Parmesan and some fresh thyme leaves just before serving.

BREXICAN

SERVES 4

PREP TIME: 15 MINS • COOK TIME: 1 HOUR

WF • GF (but check the corn chips) • V • (DF • Ve if cream and cheese are omitted)

2 tablespoons **olive oil**

2 **onions**, finely diced

1 **green pepper**, finely diced

5 cloves of **garlic**, crushed

3 × 400g tins of **black beans** (about 650g drained weight)

1.4 litres hot **vegetable stock**

1 **bay leaf**

½ teaspoon **dried oregano**

1 teaspoon **ground cumin**

1 teaspoon **chipotle paste** (optional)

2 teaspoons **cider vinegar**

2 tablespoons **lime juice**, plus a little extra to taste and to dress the topping

salt

TO SERVE:

2 **shallots**, finely diced

2 **tomatoes**, finely diced

1 **avocado**, diced

soured cream, or crumbled or **whipped feta** (see page 182) (optional)

a handful of **smashed corn chips**

This is a mash-up of a Brazilian and a Mexican soup (Brexican...), and the result is both full of flavour and packed with goodness.

Place a large heavy-based saucepan with a lid over a low heat. Add the oil and, when hot, add the onions, green pepper and salt. Sweat the vegetables gently for about 6 minutes, stirring often. Add the garlic and cook for 1 minute, then pour in the beans and hot stock, along with the bay leaf, oregano, cumin and chipotle paste, if using. Bring to the boil, then turn the heat right down, cover and simmer for 45 minutes.

By this time, the beans will have started to break apart in the soup. Fish out the bay leaf. We like to blend half the soup for a creamier texture. If, after blending, it still seems too thin, turn up the heat and reduce a little to thicken. Add the vinegar and lime juice, stir well, then taste and add more salt, lime juice or chipotle paste, if necessary.

When the soup is ready, place the diced shallot, tomato and avocado in a bowl. Squeeze over a little extra lime juice and a pinch of salt and toss. Garnish each bowl of soup with a spoonful of soured cream or feta, if using, then top with the dressed vegetables and the smashed corn chips. Serve straight away.

\\\ TIP ///

Add a small chunk of smoked bacon to the broth when you add the beans. Just before serving, shred the meat into the soup.

SPINACH, SAUSAGE & ORZO SOUP

SERVES 4

PREP TIME: 15 MINS • COOK TIME: 30 MINS

. . . .

6 plump **sausages** – look for something with lots of **onion** or **garlic**

2 tablespoons **olive oil**

1 **onion**, diced

1 **carrot**, roughly chopped

1 stick of **celery**, diced

2 cloves of **garlic**, crushed

1 tablespoon **tomato purée**

a generous pinch of **freshly grated nutmeg**

a small pinch of **dried oregano**

800ml hot **chicken** or **vegetable stock**

1 **bay leaf**

100g **orzo** or other **small pasta**

150g **spinach**, stems removed, roughly chopped

2 tablespoons **single** or **double cream**

salt and **freshly ground black pepper**

TO SERVE:
fresh parsley, chopped
fresh basil, chopped
freshly grated **Parmesan**

Orzo is the perfect pasta for soup – shaped like grains of rice, it cooks quickly in broth, taking on the flavour of the soup.

. . . .

Remove the sausage casings and shape the meat into little meatballs. Place the oil in a heavy-based pan with a lid over a medium-high heat and add the sausage meatballs. Brown them all over, then lift out and set aside. Turn the heat down to medium and add the onion, carrot, celery and a pinch of salt and pepper; sauté for 10 minutes, until soft and beginning to brown.

Add the garlic and tomato purée and cook, stirring, for 2 minutes. Next add the nutmeg, oregano, stock and bay leaf and bring to a simmer. Cook for 10 minutes.

Add the orzo, spinach and meatballs and simmer for 4 minutes, or until the orzo and meatballs are cooked. Remove from the heat, add the cream and remove the bay leaf. Taste and add more salt, freshly ground black pepper or nutmeg, if necessary.

Serve in wide bowls, with the parsley, basil and freshly grated Parmesan on top.

> ### ⟍⟍⟍ TIP ⁄⁄⁄⁄
> Orzo cooks quickly in comparison to other pastas, so serve straight away, otherwise it may become mushy. Switch the fresh herbs for a drizzle of homemade pesto (see page 186) if you fancy, or add a spoonful of aïoli (see page 174) or salsa verde (see page 180).

POSOLE

SERVES 4

PREP TIME: 30 MINS • SOAK TIME: OVERNIGHT • COOK TIME: 4 HOURS

WF · GF (but check the tostadas)

100g **dried hominy** (or 175g **cooked hominy** from a tin)

25g **dried ancho chillies**

2 **medium-hot dried red chillies**

200ml **boiling water**

6 cloves of **garlic**, crushed

500g diced **stewing pork** with some fat, ideally shoulder

1 teaspoon **ground cumin**

1 tablespoon **lard** (or **vegetable oil**)

1 **onion**, diced

1 litre hot **chicken** or **vegetable stock**

1 teaspoon **dried oregano**

1 **bay leaf**

fine salt and **freshly ground black pepper**

TO SERVE:

tostadas (see page 133)

a handful of **finely shredded white cabbage**

½ an **avocado**, diced and tossed in **lime juice**

4 **radishes**, thinly sliced

a handful of **coriander leaves**

a pinch of **dried chilli flakes**

1 **shallot**, very finely diced

Posole is a rich Mexican soup, flavoured with dried chillies and corn. Hominy is corn which has been treated with lye to change its texture and flavour, and often features in southern and North American cooking. Ancho chillies are large, dark brown dried chillies, commonly used in Mexican cooking. You can get both hominy and anchos in large supermarkets and online. John's wife Katie spent her lower sixth in Mexico and remembers eating this soup before driving around Mexico City and listening to 80s pop. Corny, and not so corny.

Soak the dried hominy in cold water overnight.

When ready to cook, place the hominy in a pan of salted water and bring to a simmer. Cook for an hour or so, while you prepare the rest of the soup.

Wearing gloves if necessary, pull apart the dried chillies and remove as much of the ribs, membranes and seeds as possible. Cover the dried chillies with the boiling water and leave to soak for 20 minutes.

Drain, but keep the soaking liquid. Place the chillies in a blender or food processor with 100ml of the liquid, a pinch of salt and 2 cloves of garlic. Process to a smooth purée, adding more of the soaking liquid to loosen if you need it, then press through a sieve to get rid of any lumpy bits. Set this hot chilli sauce to one side.

Season the pork with ½ teaspoon of fine salt and lots of freshly ground black pepper, then dust with the cumin. Toss to lightly coat each piece.

Place a wide heavy pan with a lid over a high heat and add the lard or oil. When melted, add the onion and cook for 5 minutes, stirring, until soft and beginning to brown. Next add the pork, in batches if necessary so you don't crowd the pan, and brown all over, stirring constantly. Add the remaining garlic and cook for 1 minute, then add the hot stock, oregano, bay leaf and 3 tablespoons of the ancho chilli sauce.

Drain the partly cooked hominy and add it to the soup pan. Bring to a simmer, cover partially with a lid and cook for 3 hours, stirring and checking the liquid levels every now and then.

By this point, the meat should be very tender. Retrieve the meat with a slotted spoon, draining it over the pan, and shred the dice into smaller pieces on a board, using two forks. Return the meat to the pan, adding a touch more hot water if the liquid seems too thick.

Serve the soup in warmed, deep bowls, with tostadas on the side and garnished with the shredded white cabbage, avocado, sliced radish, coriander, chilli flakes and shallot.

\\\ TIP ///

Be patient with this soup – the corn should be very tender and the pork melt-in-the-mouth, so it can't be rushed.

TIP

At LEON, we serve this with a drizzle of pesto on top.

SICILIAN-STYLE
SPICY CHICKEN MEATBALL

SERVES 4

PREP TIME: 20 MINS · COOK TIME: 40 MINS

3 tablespoons **olive oil**

1 fat clove of **garlic**, crushed to a paste

2 × 400g tins **chopped tomatoes**

½ teaspoon **chilli flakes**, or to taste

250ml hot **vegetable stock**

200g **macaroni** or **ditalini**

150ml **boiling water**

salt and **freshly ground black pepper**

fresh parsley, chopped, to serve

freshly grated **Parmesan cheese**, to serve

FOR THE MEATBALLS:

1 slice of **stale bread**, crusts removed

4 tablespoons **milk**

450g **minced chicken** or **chicken breasts**, minced in a food processor

½ teaspoon **fennel seeds**

½ teaspoon **chilli flakes**

2 tablespoons **pine nuts**

1 heaped tablespoon **roughly chopped sultanas**

zest of ½ a **lemon**, grated

2 tablespoons **finely chopped fresh parsley**

2 tablespoons **capers**, drained and rinsed, roughly chopped

2 cloves of **garlic**, crushed to a paste

2 tablespoons **olive oil**

a knob of **butter**

We love these chicken meatballs, studded with pine nuts, fennel seeds and capers, simmered in a spicy tomato broth. This soup is inspired by our Sicilian Meatball Hot Box, created by John's friend Scott Uehlien, who was Head of Food at the US retreat Canyon Ranch. Thanks, Scott.

First, make the soup. Place the oil, garlic, tomatoes, chilli flakes, stock and some salt and pepper in a large heavy-based pan with a lid. Bring to a simmer, then cover and cook until the tomatoes have broken down and are pulpy, around 20–30 minutes.

Meanwhile, make the meatballs. Use a food processor to turn the bread into crumbs (or crumble into tiny pieces with your hands). Then stir through the milk to soften.

Tip the minced chicken and milky breadcrumbs into a bowl and add a pinch of salt and a generous amount of ground black pepper. Place the fennel seeds, chilli flakes and pine nuts in a hot dry pan and toast briefly, stirring, until golden, then add to the bowl with the sultanas, lemon zest, parsley, capers and garlic. Use your hands to mix everything together, then shape into 20 balls, each around 3cm in diameter.

Place the oil and butter in a frying pan set over a medium heat. Add the meatballs and brown them all over. (Once one side has browned, turn the balls sideways, as turning them right over allows them to flatten out and lose their round shape.)

The pasta and meatballs now cook in the soup: the meatballs need about 10 minutes, while the pasta will depend on which variety you choose. Add the boiling water to the pan, stir, then add the meatballs and then the pasta, according to its cooking time.

Cover the pan, but stir every minute or two to prevent the pasta and sauce sticking to the bottom and burning.

When the pasta is cooked, remove from the heat. Serve topped with the fresh parsley and lots of freshly grated Parmesan.

CREAM OF CHICKEN

SERVES 4
PREP TIME: 10 MINS • COOK TIME: 1 HOUR

a generous knob of **butter**

4 **chicken thighs**, bone in, skin removed

2 **onions**, diced

2 **leeks**, trimmed and finely chopped

2 tablespoons **plain flour**

1 litre hot **chicken stock**

1 **bay leaf**

2 sprigs of **fresh thyme**

3 whole **fresh parsley sprigs**

100–150ml **single cream**

salt and **freshly ground black pepper**

garlicky croutons (see page 196), or **hot buttered toast**, to serve

A soup for rainy, bleary, coldy days – guaranteed to make you feel better. We like to make vats of it, and freeze single portions so it's always on hand if anyone is ill or under the weather.

Place a large heavy-based pan with a lid over a medium heat. Add the butter and, when foaming, add the chicken thighs. Brown all over, then remove and set aside. In the same pan, sweat the onions and leeks until soft, about 10 minutes. Add the flour to the pan and stir, cooking for a couple of minutes. Next, add the hot stock and return the chicken thighs to the pan. Add the bay leaf, thyme and parsley sprigs, and some salt and pepper, then turn the heat down to a simmer and cover.

Cook for 45 minutes, until the thigh meat is cooked through and really tender. Remove from the pan and pull the meat from the bones, using a couple of forks. Discard the bones and return the meat to the pan. Simmer for a further 5 minutes, then remove from the heat. Fish the herbs out and discard. Add the cream and blend until smooth.

Taste and adjust the seasoning if necessary.

Serve with garlic croutons on top, or hot buttered toast on the side.

\\\ TIP ///

Add a handful of sliced, cooked mushrooms for the last 5 minutes of cooking, reserving a few for a garnish.

KEN'S TONKOTSU RAMEN

SERVES 6

PREP TIME: 30 MINS • MARINATING TIME: OVERNIGHT • COOK TIME: 30 MINS for the soup + 10 HOURS for the stock

DF

FOR THE TONKOTSU STOCK:

2 **pig's trotters**

1kg **pig bones** – we use **backbones** and **shinbones**

500g **rolled pork belly**

200g **pork back fat** (lardo)

a couple of **chicken's feet**, or a **chicken carcass**

2 **onions**, peeled and quartered

2 **spring onions**, quartered

4 cloves of **garlic**, peeled

5-cm piece of **fresh ginger**, roughly chopped

15-cm piece of **kombu**

Rebecca's friends Ken Yamada and Emma Reynolds co-founded Tonkotsu, one of London's first and most beloved ramen noodle joints, in 2012. This is their tonkotsu-at-home recipe. It is a relatively easy dish to assemble but is best split over two days, as the stock takes many hours boiling to get its rich, collagen and lip-smacking porky fattiness. Don't be put off; most of the time it needs little more than a stir every half an hour.

This is the opposite of making clear French stock: rather than skimming off the fat, the aim is to emulsify it into the stock for a creamy, white consistency. Your butcher should be able to get the bones and fat for you; kombu seaweed, dashi, mirin and rice wine vinegar are all available from Japanese or Asian supermarkets and online.

It is important that the fat amalgamates itself into this stock. To do this, and to prevent the stock from splitting, you need to boil vigorously with the lid on, in order to raise the pressure in the pan.

Put the trotters and pig bones into your largest pan with a lid – you need room for all the ingredients. Add boiling water, covering the bones by a few centimetres, and boil vigorously with the lid on for 5 hours. Skim the froth from the surface every now and then and keep an eye on the water level, adding more boiling water when necessary.

Add the pork belly roll and the back fat to the pan. Meanwhile, start the soy base (recipe overleaf). After 3 further hours boiling, remove the pork belly. Rest it on a tray for an hour, then submerge it in 1.75 litres of the soy base to marinate.

Add the chicken feet or carcass, the vegetables, garlic and ginger to the broth and bring back to a vigorous boil, with the lid on. After a further 2 hours of boiling, remove the pan from the heat and add the kombu.

Cool for at least an hour, or until cool enough to handle. Sieve the bones and vegetables out, retaining and refrigerating the rich white stock.

\\\\ TIP ////

This recipe makes 3 litres of stock, but if you want to multiply the quantities (you will need a big pan!) it freezes well too.

KEN'S TONKOTSU RAMEN
(CONTINUED)

FOR THE MARINATED EGGS:

1 **egg** per person, at room temperature

200ml **soy base** (recipe below)

1 teaspoon **dashi powder**

200ml **water**

Bring a pan of water to the boil. Before placing the eggs in the pan, given them a shake for 3 seconds to centralize the yolk. Place up to 6 eggs (no more per pan) into a noodle sieve or metal colander and lower it into the boiling water for exactly 6 minutes and 10 seconds.

Remove the eggs from the pan and plunge them into a bowl of cold water with the cold tap running into it – this is to stop the eggs cooking further. When cooled, tap the eggs all over with a spoon to crack the shells. Carefully peel, keeping them under cold water. When the eggs are completely cold, mix the soy base, dashi and water together and place the eggs in this marinade. Marinate overnight in the fridge.

FOR THE SOY BASE (MAKES 2 LITRES):

160ml **cooking sake**

12g **salt**

50g **granulated sugar**

900ml **dark soy sauce**

3 cloves of **garlic**

30g chunk of **fresh ginger**

5 **spring onions**

900ml **water**

Combine all the ingredients in a large pan and place over a low to medium heat. Warm until the salt and sugar have dissolved. Don't boil.

When cooled, take 250ml of base and dilute it with 250ml of water.

Once the eggs (above) are cooked, use this mixture to marinate them.

Use the rest of the soy base to marinate the pork belly from the tonkotsu stock (see page 65).

FOR THE SALT BASE (MAKES 200ML):

150ml **water**

7½-cm piece of **kombu**

20g **sea salt**

30ml **sake**

10ml **mirin**

10ml **rice vinegar**

1 teaspoon **soy sauce**

Place all the ingredients in a pan and warm over a low heat until the salt has dissolved. Stir occasionally and make sure it doesn't boil. Set aside to cool.

TO SERVE THE TONKOTSU RAMEN (SERVES 6):

2.1 litres **tonkotsu stock** (see page 65)

500g **marinated cooked pork belly** (see page 65)

400g **beansprouts**

6 portions of **noodles** (fresh wheat noodles are best, but dried are fine)

150ml **salt base** (see opposite)

200g **spring onions**, finely chopped

6 **marinated eggs**, halved (see opposite)

2 tablespoons **white sesame seeds**

Heat the tonkotsu stock until boiling. Cut the pork belly into 12 slices, then reheat and crisp slightly under a hot grill.

Bring a pan of water to the boil and blanch the beansprouts for 20 seconds, then drain.

In a separate pan, cook the noodles for 10 seconds less than the packet instructions suggest.

To serve, place 25ml of the salt base and 350ml of the tonkotsu stock in each serving bowl. Add the noodles as soon as they are cooked, then top with 2 slices of pork belly per bowl, the beansprouts, spring onions, halved eggs, and a pinch of white sesame seeds.

Slurp immediately!

CELERIAC & CRISPY SAGE

SERVES 4

PREP TIME: 10 MINS • COOK TIME: 45 MINS

WF · GF (if croutons are omitted) • (V · Ve if made with vegetable stock)

2 knobs of **butter**

1 **onion**, diced

1 **leek**, finely sliced

200g **floury white potatoes**, about
    2 medium potatoes, peeled and diced

1 head of **celeriac**, peeled and
    roughly diced

1 litre hot **chicken** or **vegetable stock**

20 **fresh sage leaves**

1 sprig of **fresh thyme**

1 tablespoon **olive oil**

croutons (see page 196), to serve

For years, whenever a celeriac turned up in Rebecca's veg box, all she could think of was remoulade – and one celeriac makes a lot of remoulade. This soup is a much better way to turn the knobbly veg into something silky and delicious.

Place 1 knob of the butter into a large heavy-based pan with a lid over a medium heat. When foaming, add the onion and leek and sweat for 8 minutes. As soon as they start to brown, add the potatoes, celeriac, stock, 5 of the sage leaves and the thyme. Bring to a simmer, then cover and leave to cook for 25–35 minutes, or until the celeriac is very tender.

Remove the herbs from the soup and blend it until smooth, working in batches if necessary.

To make the crispy sage leaf garnish, pour the olive oil and remaining knob of butter into a small pan and set it over a medium heat. Pat the remaining sage leaves dry if necessary, then drop them into the hot fat for 10–15 seconds only, turning once. Lift out and drain on kitchen paper.

Serve the soup garnished with the crispy leaves and some croutons.

BLACK DAL

SERVES 4
PREP TIME: 15 MINS · SOAK TIME: 8 HOURS · COOK TIME: 6 HOURS
(WF · GF if bread is omitted) · V

200g **dried black lentils (urid/urad dal)**

750ml **hot water**, plus more
    during cooking

3 knobs of **butter**

5 **cloves**

4 **green cardamom pods**

¼ teaspoon **fennel seeds**

½ teaspoon **cumin seeds**

1 teaspoon **garam masala**

¼ teaspoon **ground cinnamon**

¼ teaspoon **chilli powder**

a piece of **fresh ginger**, grated

2 cloves of **garlic**, crushed

½ a **fresh green chilli**, seeded and
    finely chopped

1 **onion**, finely chopped

1 tablespoon **tomato purée**

1 **bay leaf**

1 teaspoon **brown sugar**

100g **tinned kidney beans** (about
    ½ a tin), drained and rinsed

4 tablespoons **double cream**

salt and **freshly ground black pepper**

TO SERVE:
fresh **coriander**
chapatis, **naan**, **parthas** or **popadoms**

This very, very slow-cooked black lentil dish from the Punjab is rich and smoky, and as it cooks the lentils become deliciously soft and creamy. Although the cooking time is lengthy, it needs very little attention and the end result is really special. Dedicated to Dar Barot and Sumi Jeffrey for reasons we can explain if we ever meet.

Soak the lentils for 8 hours or overnight in cold water. Drain and rinse in fresh water.

Transfer to a ovenproof pan with a lid and add the hot water. Bring to a fast boil and cook for 5 minutes. Turn the heat down, skim off any scum that forms on the surface, then cover and cook until the lentils are soft and beginning to break down, which will take 30–40 minutes.

Meanwhile, in a separate pan over a low heat, melt the first knob of butter and add the cloves, cardamom pods, fennel seeds, cumin seeds, garam masala, cinnamon and chilli powder. Cook, stirring, for a couple of minutes, then add the ginger and garlic, and cook for a minute or two longer. Add the second knob of butter, green chilli and onion, along with a pinch of salt and the tomato purée, and cook for about 10 minutes, stirring often, until the onion is soft. Remove from the heat, add the bay leaf, sugar and a grinding of black pepper, and set aside until the lentils are ready.

When the lentils are soft, heat the oven to 160°C/325°F/gas mark 3. Roughly mash the kidney beans and add to the lentils with the spiced onions, then cover with the lid. Place in the preheated oven and cook for 4–5 hours, or even longer if you can, adding 3 or 4 tablespoons of water every hour so, and stirring the contents of the pan to prevent sticking.

When ready, the dal will be very creamy, and the longer you leave it, the deeper brown it will go. Remove from the oven and stir in the cream and the final knob of

butter, plus enough hot water to loosen the dal until it forms a thick soup. Taste and add a little more salt, if necessary. Remove the bay leaf and cardamom pods, if you can find them, before serving. Garnish with a little fresh coriander.

Eat with wedges of Indian flatbread – chapatis, naan or parathas are all good – or dunk popadoms into the soup.

\\\ TIP ///

Serve with the raita on page 171. Urid/urad dal is easy to find in Asian supermarkets and online – just make sure you choose the black variety, rather than the white.

MULLIGATAWNY

SERVES 4

PREP TIME: 15 MINS • COOK TIME: 1 HOUR

WF • GF (if flatbread is omitted)

a knob of **butter**

2 tablespoons **vegetable oil**

300g boneless, skinless **chicken thighs**, cut into rough 1-cm pieces

1 **onion**, finely diced

1 stick of **celery**, finely diced

1 **carrot**, roughly chopped

2-cm piece of **fresh ginger**, peeled and grated

2 cloves of **garlic**, crushed

1 small tart **green apple**, peeled, cored and diced

1 tablespoon **curry powder** (we use Madras)

1 litre hot good-quality **chicken stock**

100g **split red lentils**, rinsed

3 tablespoons **coconut milk** or
   1 tablespoon **single cream**

2 teaspoons fresh **lemon juice**

¼–½ teaspoon **cayenne pepper**, to taste (optional)

salt and **freshly ground black pepper**

TO SERVE:

coriander leaves

naan or other **Indian flatbread**

plain or **garlic yoghurt** (see page 170)

This retro soup dates back to the British Raj, when Indian cooks invented it for their soup-loving colonial masters. We love it with chicken, but you can use lamb instead (just give it a longer, slower cook until tender). Vegetarians can make an excellent version with butternut squash or sweet potatoes instead, added to simmer along with the lentils.

Place the butter and oil in a large heavy-based pan with a lid, set over a medium heat. When foaming, add the chicken, working in batches so as not to crowd the pan, and brown lightly all over. Remove and set aside, then add the onion, celery and carrot, and cook, stirring, for about 10 minutes, until the onion is translucent, but not brown.

Add the ginger and garlic and cook for a minute, then add the apple, some black pepper and the curry powder and cook for another minute, stirring again. Pour in the hot stock and return the chicken to the pan along with the lentils. Bring to a merry boil for a couple of minutes, skimming off any scum or foam, then turn the heat right down and simmer for 30 minutes, until the lentils are collapsing and the chicken is very tender.

Remove from the heat, add the coconut milk or cream, and blend half the soup until smooth, leaving the other half chunky and textured. Mix together.

Taste the soup and add half the lemon juice, then taste again and add the rest, with some salt, if liked (some curry powders contain salt, so you may not need any more). If you'd like a more potent soup, add the cayenne pepper and simmer for a couple more minutes.

Serve garnished with coriander leaves, with some flatbreads and yoghurt on the side.

＼＼\ TIP /／／

Serve with raita (see page 171) or labneh (see page 183). Make a heartier soup (and one great for lunchboxes) by adding 4 tablespoons of uncooked basmati rice to the blended soup, then simmering until cooked. Reheat thoroughly.

TUSCAN WHITE BEAN & KALE WITH SAUSAGE

SERVES 4
PREP TIME: 10 MINS • COOK TIME: 45 MINS
(WF • GF if bread is omitted, but check the sausages) • DF

1 tablespoon **vegetable oil**

400g **garlicky pork sausages**, about
   6 sausages, chopped into ½-cm pieces

1 **onion**, finely chopped plus 2 **onions**,
   sliced into rounds

1 **carrot**, finely chopped

1 stick of **celery**, finely chopped

1 clove of **garlic**, crushed

1 teaspoon **tomato purée**

100ml **passata**

750ml high-quality hot **chicken** or
   vegetable stock

1 **bay leaf**

3-cm sprig of **rosemary**

2 sprigs of **fresh thyme**

400g tin of **cannellini beans**, drained
   and rinsed (230g cooked beans)

100g **kale**, ribs removed, shredded

salt and **freshly ground black pepper**

crusty bread, to serve

An easy soup to warm your cockles in the depths of winter, giving some much-needed nutrients, too.

Place a large heavy-based saucepan with a lid over a high heat. Add the oil and when hot, tip the sausage pieces in. Cook, moving them around in the pan, until browned all over and cooked through. Lift out of the pan, set aside the sausage, turn the heat to low and add the onion, carrot, celery and a pinch of salt. Sweat the vegetables gently for about 10 minutes, stirring often.

Add the garlic and tomato purée and cook, stirring, for a minute. Pour in the passata and hot stock, then add the bay leaf, rosemary and thyme, plus a good grinding of black pepper. Stir, bring to a simmer, then cover and leave to cook for about 20 minutes, or until the vegetables are tender.

Add the cannellini beans, kale and reserved cooked sausage to the pan, and cook for 3 or 4 minutes. Remove the herbs and serve with crusty bread to mop up the broth.

\\\\ TIP ////

A little gremolata (see page 179) on top gives this earthy soup a fresh-flavoured facelift. For a real meal in a bowl, add 200g pasta to the broth for the last 10 minutes of cooking. The sausages can easily be left out for vegetarians.

RED LENTILS WITH SPINACH, YOGHURT, POMEGRANATE & CRISPY ONIONS

SERVES 4

PREP TIME: 15 MINS • COOK TIME: 50 MINS

WF • GF • V • Ve (if yoghurt is omitted)

. . . .

1 tablespoon **vegetable oil**

1 **onion**, finely chopped

1 **carrot**, finely chopped

1 stick of **celery**, finely chopped

1 teaspoon **cumin seeds**

1 teaspoon **coriander seeds**

1 clove of **garlic**, crushed

1.25 litres good-quality hot
   vegetable stock

200g **split red lentils**, rinsed

150g **baby leaf spinach**, roughly chopped

salt

TO SERVE:

4 tablespoons **Greek yoghurt**

crispy onions (see page 193)

4 tablespoons **pomegranate seeds**

Pomegranate seeds sit like little jewels on top of this Turkish-inspired soup.

. . . .

Place a large heavy-based saucepan with a lid over a medium-low heat. Add the oil, onion, carrot, celery and a pinch of salt, and sweat the vegetables gently for about 10 minutes, stirring often.

Meanwhile, toast the cumin and coriander seeds for a couple of minutes in a hot dry pan until fragrant, then tip into a pestle and mortar and grind to a powder.

As the vegetables begin to brown, add the garlic to the pan and cook for 1 minute, stirring, then add the ground spices, hot stock and the lentils. Bring to a fast boil and leave for 3 or 4 minutes, then turn the heat down to a simmer and skim any scum which has formed on top of the liquid. Cover and simmer for 20–25 minutes, until the lentils are completely soft.

Remove the soup from the heat and blend until completely smooth. Taste and add a little more seasoning if necessary. If the soup seems too thick, add a splash of hot water to thin it.

To serve, return the soup to the pan and add the spinach. Stir it in and allow it to wilt, then divide the soup between 4 bowls. Top each with a spoonful of yoghurt, the crispy onions and the pomegranate seeds.

\\\\ TIP ////

This is very adaptable: swap the yoghurt for tahini with mint (see page 172), harissa (see page 173), zhoug (see page 181), labneh (see page 183) or whipped feta (see page 182); or switch the pomegranate for chopped fresh red chilli.

WINTERY TOMATO SOUP

SERVES 4

PREP TIME: 10 MINS • COOK TIME: 40 MINS

V (if made with vegetable stock) • (WF • GF • DF • Ve if posh four-cheese toasties are omitted)

1 tablespoon **olive oil**

2 **onions**, diced

2 **carrots**, diced

2 sticks of **celery**, diced

2 cloves of **garlic**, crushed

1 tablespoon **tomato purée**

2 × 400g tins **chopped tomatoes**

1 teaspoon **balsamic vinegar**

2 heaped teaspoons **soft brown sugar**

700ml hot **chicken** or **vegetable stock**

salt and **freshly ground black pepper**

posh four-cheese toasties
   (see page 208), to serve

In the winter, if you've got a craving for tomato soup, it's best to use tinned tomatoes as fresh tomatoes will be flavourless at this time of year. We love this soup as it is, tart and zingy, but if you like a cream of tomato soup, add 2 tablespoons of double cream to the soup after blending.

Set a large heavy-based pan with a lid over a medium heat. Add the oil, onion, carrot, celery and a generous pinch of salt and cook gently for 10 minutes. Add the garlic and tomato purée and continue to cook for 4 minutes, stirring constantly. Don't allow the vegetables to brown.

Add the tomatoes and their juices from the tin, the vinegar, sugar, some black pepper and the hot stock. Bring up to a simmer, cover and leave to cook for 30 minutes, stirring occasionally.

Blend the soup until completely smooth, in batches if necessary. Taste and add more seasoning if necessary.

Serve with posh four-cheese toasties.

TOM KHA GAI

SERVES 4 as a starter, or 2 as a main meal
PREP TIME: 10 MINS • COOK TIME: 25 MINS
WF · GF · DF

400ml **full-fat coconut milk**

275ml hot **chicken stock**

350g **skinless, boneless chicken thighs**,
cut into 1-cm strips

3-cm piece of **galangal**, roughly chopped

1 stick of **lemongrass**, trimmed
and bruised

4 **lime leaves**, stems removed, torn
into pieces

2 **hot red chillies**, seeded and finely
sliced (or to taste)

¼-cm slice of **fresh ginger**, peeled

½ teaspoon **dried red chilli flakes**

a pinch of **fine salt**

½ teaspoon **brown sugar**

100g **oyster mushrooms**, torn into bite-
sized pieces

1½ tablespoons **fish sauce** (or more
to taste)

juice of ½ a **lime** (or more to taste)

coriander leaves from 8 sprigs, to serve

This tangy, hot and sour Thai soup is like a creamier version of tom yum (see page 22), and is often served with white rice on the side.

Pour the coconut milk and chicken stock into a large saucepan and place over a low heat. Slowly and gently bring to a low boil – doing this slowly helps stop the coconut milk from splitting.

Add the chicken, galangal, lemongrass, lime leaves, chillies (reserving a little for garnish), ginger, chilli flakes, salt and sugar, bring back to a simmer and cook for 6 minutes. Add the mushrooms and cook for a further 3 minutes. Check the chicken is cooked through, then remove from the heat and stir in the fish sauce and lime juice. Taste and add more of either, if you like.

Serve garnished with the reserved chillies and the coriander leaves.

\ \ \ \ TIP / / / ,

As with the tom yum (yum yum) on page 22, you could add some Thai roasted chilli paste, *nam phrik phao*, for extra heat and colour, or homemade sweet chilli sauce (see page 176); or swap the chicken for seafood, fish or vegetables.

PANCOTTO

SERVES 2

PREP TIME: 10 MINS • COOK TIME: 25 MINS

V

2 tablespoons **olive oil**

½ an **onion**, finely diced

1 stick of **celery**, finely diced

1 **carrot**, roughly chopped

2 cloves of **garlic**, whole

pinch of **dried red chilli flakes**,
   or to taste

450ml **hot water**

150g slightly stale, firm, **crusty
   white bread**, crusts removed

a little **Pecorino**, freshly grated

salt and **freshly ground black pepper**

TO SERVE:

good-quality **extra virgin olive oil**

lots of **Pecorino**, freshly grated

a handful of **chopped fresh herbs** – any
   combination of **oregano**, **marjoram**,
   basil and **parsley**

> \\\\ **TIP** ////
>
> For a punchier flavour, add a
> spoonful of salsa verde (see
> page 180) to each bowl.

There are dozens of Italian bread soup recipes, as Italian cooks sensibly consider it a shocking waste to throw away stale bread. The simplest are made with just bread, water, olive oil, salt, pepper and cheese, perhaps with an egg whisked through at the end. More complex versions use beef broth, tomatoes, pancetta, green beans, courgettes or potatoes. This is our take on the traditional Tuscan pancotto – a soft, calming, porridge-like soup.

Place the oil in a large heavy-based saucepan with a lid, set over a medium heat. When hot, add the onion, celery, carrot, whole cloves of garlic and a pinch of salt, and cook, stirring, for about 10 minutes, until the onion is translucent, but not brown. Next, add the chilli flakes, hot water and the bread, torn into small pieces. Season with plenty of black pepper, then cook gently, stirring often to prevent sticking, for about 10 minutes, or until the bread has broken down completely and the carrots are tender. Grate a little Pecorino over the top and stir it in. Add more water if the soup seems too thick – it should be like porridge. Taste and add more seasoning if necessary, then remove the garlic.

Rest the soup, covered, for 5 minutes before serving. Serve each portion topped with a spoonful of extra virgin olive oil, more Pecorino and black pepper, and a little tangle of fresh herbs.

PEARLY KING (OF SOUPS)

SERVES 4

PREP TIME: 15 MINS · COOK TIME: up to 3 HOURS

DF

. . . .

1 tablespoon **cooking oil**

400g **lamb neck fillet**, or other stewing **lamb** or **mutton**, in small dice

1 **onion**, diced

2 **carrots**, diced

2 **leeks**, sliced

2 sticks of **celery**, diced

1 **swede**, peeled and cut into 2-cm chunks

1.5 litres hot **chicken** or **vegetable stock**

3-cm sprig of **fresh rosemary**

1 **bay leaf**

6 tablespoons **uncooked pearl barley**

150g shredded **green cabbage (Savoy, pointed** or **spring greens** all work well)

salt and **freshly ground black pepper**

TO SERVE:

2 tablespoons **finely chopped fresh parsley**

crusty bread

A warming soup ideal for simmering on the stove on a cosy, lazy Sunday afternoon. You can make this using leftover roast lamb, just add the meat and bones to the pan with the stock and cook for 20 minutes, then add the pearl barley and remove the bones before serving. If you prefer beef to lamb, just swap for stewing beef.

. . . .

Place a large heavy-based saucepan with a lid over a high heat. Add the cooking oil and when hot, add the diced lamb. Brown thoroughly, then remove from the pan and set aside, leaving the fat behind. Add the onion and a pinch of salt, and cook for 5 minutes, then turn the heat down to medium and add the carrots, leeks and celery. Allow the vegetables to sweat for about 10 minutes, stirring regularly, then add the swede and cook for a couple of minutes longer.

Return the meat to the pan and pour in the hot stock, along with the rosemary and bay leaf. Bring to a simmer, cover, then turn the heat right down and leave to cook for an hour.

Meanwhile, if the pearl barley requires rinsing or pre-boiling, do so now. When the broth has been cooking for an hour, add the pearl barley and cook until tender, anywhere from 45 minutes to an hour and a half. While the barley is cooking, check the lamb – it should be meltingly tender.

When ready to serve, add the cabbage, turn up the heat, cover and cook for 3 minutes, until the cabbage is just tender but still has some bite. Add a little more water for a thinner consistency, if necessary. Taste and add a little more salt and some freshly ground black pepper. Garnish with the parsley.

Serve in wide bowls, with crusty bread to mop up the juices.

CHICKPEA, SWEET POTATO & CHORIZO

SERVES 4
PREP TIME: 10 MINS • COOK TIME: 50 MINS
WF • GF (but check the sausages) • DF

1 tablespoon **olive oil**

200g **cooking chorizo**, diced

1 **onion**, finely chopped

1 **carrot**, finely chopped

1 stick of **celery**, finely chopped

1 clove of **garlic**, crushed

1 teaspoon **tomato purée**

400g **sweet potatoes**, about 3 medium potatoes, peeled and cut into 1-cm dice

1 litre good-quality hot **chicken** or **vegetable stock**

400g tin of **chickpeas**, drained and rinsed (or 230g cooked chickpeas)

1 teaspoon **sweet** or **hot smoked paprika**

salt and **freshly ground black pepper**

fresh coriander leaves, to serve

Sweet potato is a natural partner for smoky chorizo in this Spanish-style soup.

Place a large heavy-based saucepan with a lid over a medium heat. Add the oil and the diced cooking chorizo and sauté until the sausage is browned. Lift the meat out of the pan and set aside, leaving the red oil behind.

Add the onion, carrot and celery to the pan, along with a pinch of salt, then turn the heat to low and sweat the vegetables gently for about 10 minutes, stirring often. As they begin to brown, add the garlic and tomato purée and cook for 1 minute, stirring, then add the diced sweet potatoes. Add the hot stock and a good grinding of black pepper, bring to a simmer, and then cover. Turn the heat right down and cook until the sweet potatoes are tender but not mushy, 20–30 minutes.

Tip the chickpeas into the pan along with the smoked paprika, stir and simmer for a couple of minutes to heat through. Use a ladle to scoop out half the mixture and blend until smooth, then return to the pan. Taste and add a little more salt, pepper or paprika, if necessary.

To serve, heat through the reserved chorizo and scatter a quarter of it over each bowl, along with the coriander leaves.

\\\\ TIP ////

For extra heat, garnish with chopped fresh chilli. For an even heartier soup, top with a poached egg or some aioli (see page 174).

ROASTED SQUASH

SERVES 4 as a starter, or 2 as a hearty lunch
PREP TIME: 10 MINS • COOK TIME: 50 MINS
WF • GF • DF • V • Ve

1 large **butternut squash** or medium
    pumpkin, peeled, seeded and cut into
    large chunks

1 **onion**, cut into 6 chunks

3 cloves of **garlic**, in their skins

flavourless oil

2-cm piece of **fresh ginger**, grated

600ml hot **vegetable stock**

a generous pinch of **freshly
    grated nutmeg**

½ teaspoon **sweet smoked paprika**

a pinch of **dried red chilli flakes**

freshly squeezed **lime juice**

salt and **freshly ground black pepper**

puffed and popped seeds
    (see page 191), to serve

\\\\ TIP ////

Squash marries well with cumin
and coriander – see the carrot
soup on page 12 and steal the
spicing from that one, instead
of nutmeg and paprika, and add
some fresh coriander leaves
to serve. Or, toss a handful of
freshly made gremolata (see
page 179) over each bowl.

---

*Roasting the squash or pumpkin brings out its natural creamy sweetness,
but also makes this a very hands-off and simple vegan soup to make.
For a more savoury note to this slightly sweet soup, add some crispy sage
leaves (see the celeriac and crispy sage soup on page 69) or a handful of
nutty spiced dukkah (see page 190), as a topping.*

Heat the oven to 200°C/400°F/gas mark 6.

Place the squash or pumpkin chunks, onion pieces and whole garlic cloves in a large roasting tin and splash over a little flavourless oil plus some salt and pepper. Toss everything to coat, then pop into the oven and roast for 45 minutes.

Remove from the oven and set aside. When cool enough, squeeze the roasted garlic from the skins, and discard the skins. Pick out any shards of onion that look particularly leathery.

Meanwhile, in a large saucepan with a lid, sauté the ginger for a minute in a little more of the oil, then add the stock, nutmeg, paprika and chilli flakes and the roasted vegetables, leaving the cooking oil behind in the tin. Bring to a simmer for just a minute, then remove from the heat and blend until smooth (a jug blender is best for this soup, in which case work in batches).

Taste the soup and add a little lime juice, just a teaspoon at a time. It may need more salt, pepper or spice, and you may want to thin it with a little hot water or stock if it is really thick.

Serve with puffed and popped seeds on top.

SPLIT PEA

SERVES 4

PREP TIME: 10 MINS • SOAK TIME: OVERNIGHT • COOK TIME: up to 2 HOURS

WF • GF • V • (**DF • Ve** if butter is omitted)

200g **yellow split peas**

1 tablespoon **olive oil**

1 **onion**, diced

1 **carrot**, diced

1 **leek**, finely sliced

1 stick of **celery**, finely diced

2 cloves of **garlic**, crushed

1.25 litres hot **vegetable stock**

1 teaspoon **sweet smoked paprika**

1 teaspoon **lemon juice**

salt and **freshly ground black pepper**

knob of **butter** (optional)

Traditionally split pea soup is made with bacon or ham hocks (like the Puy lentils, bacon & mustard cream on page 41), but this is a vegetarian version. The smoked paprika lends the smokiness normally found in the smoked pork. We reckon using yellow split peas results in a more appetizing soup than the murky-coloured green ones. You can speed up the cooking process by using a pressure cooker, if you have one.

Soak the split peas in cold water for 8 hours or overnight. When ready to cook, drain the peas, rinse in a couple of changes of fresh water and drain again.

Put the oil into a large saucepan with a lid, set over a medium heat. Add the onion, carrot, leek and celery and cook for about 10 minutes, until the onion is beginning to become translucent. Add the garlic and cook for 1 minute, then add the soaked split peas and the hot stock.

Turn the heat up and bring to a fast boil. Allow to boil rapidly for 10 minutes, skimming off any foam or scum that forms on top of the broth.

After 10 minutes, turn the heat down and cover the pan with a lid. Simmer gently for 1–1½ hours, or longer if necessary, until the split peas are soft. You may need to add more hot water every now and then if the soup becomes too dry. Remove from the heat and blend until completely smooth.

Return the soup to the pan, place over a low heat and add the smoked paprika and lemon juice along with enough hot water to thin the soup to your preferred consistency. Taste and add salt and freshly ground pepper as necessary.

Finish by stirring through the knob of butter, if using.

\\\ TIP ///

This earthy soup is good with some salty, crunchy corn chips sprinkled over it, a dollop of labneh (see page 183) or aïoli (see page 174), or a drizzle of lemon and some chilli oil (see page 177).

RIBOLLITA

SERVES 2

PREP TIME: 10 MINS · COOK TIME: 35 MINS

V · DF · Ve (if cheese is omitted)

1 tablespoon **olive oil**

½ an **onion**, diced

1 stick of **celery**, diced

1 **carrot**, diced

2 cloves of **garlic**, crushed

2 sprigs of **fresh thyme**

1 teaspoon **tomato purée**

1 medium **tomato**, seeded and chopped

500ml weak, hot **vegetable stock**

400g tin of **cannellini beans** (about 230g drained weight), drained and rinsed

100g shredded **kale**, **chard** or **Savoy cabbage**, or a mixture, ribs and stems removed

1 large or 2 medium slices of firm, slightly stale **wholewheat** or **good-quality white bread**

freshly ground black pepper

TO SERVE:

extra virgin olive oil

lots of grated **Pecorino** or **Parmesan**

Hearty and bursting with goodness, this bread, bean and kale soup is even better the next day. For a truly authentic Tuscan ribollita, you should soak 100g dried beans overnight then simmer for several hours until cooked before using (but we think tinned beans are a lot easier).

Place the oil in a large heavy-based saucepan with a lid, set over a medium heat. When hot, add the onion, celery and carrot, and cook gently, stirring often, for about 10 minutes, until the onion is translucent. Don't brown the vegetables. Add the garlic, thyme, tomato purée and chopped tomato, stir and cook for a minute, then add the hot stock.

Blend a quarter of the drained beans with a little water, until smooth. When the broth is simmering, add the whole and puréed cannellini beans, the greens and a grinding of black pepper to the pan and stir again. We like our greens to have a bit of bite, but traditionally they are cooked for a fairly long time – up to an hour. We go for 15 minutes, tops.

Tear the bread into pieces and add to the pan. Cook for a couple of minutes until soft.

Serve in wide soup bowls, with a spoonful of extra virgin olive oil drizzled over, and lots of freshly grated Pecorino on top.

\\\ TIP ///

The cooked bread inevitably gives this soup a soft texture; if you don't like this, serve the bread as toast alongside, or serve the soup with the posh four-cheese toasties on page 208. A dollop of aïoli (see page 174) or salsa verde (see page 180) would posh up this peasant soup.

CAULIFLOWER & CHICKPEAS

SERVES 4

PREP TIME: 10 MINS • COOK TIME: 40 MINS

WF • GF • V • (DF • Ve if cream, yoghurt and crème fraîche are omitted)

1 head of **cauliflower**, broken into florets

1 **onion**, sliced into half moons

1 teaspoon **ground cumin**

1 teaspoon **paprika**

3 tablespoons **olive oil**

150g **floury potatoes**, about 1 medium potato, peeled and cut into medium pieces

1 litre hot **vegetable stock**

2 cloves of **garlic**, sliced

400g tin of **chickpeas**, drained and rinsed

zest of ½ a **lemon**, plus 1 tablespoon of **lemon juice**

salt and **freshly ground black pepper**

TO SERVE:

single cream, **Greek-style yoghurt** or **crème fraîche** (optional)

1 tablespoon **cumin seeds**, lightly toasted

At first glance, cauliflower soup might not sound like the best idea, but this is incredibly good and cauliflower has the added bonus of being a rare source of vital vitamin K. For an Indian-style vegan soup, leave out the paprika but add a teaspoonful of garam masala, 2cm of ginger, finely grated, and a pinch of ground chilli, and finish with a swirl of unsweetened coconut milk.

Heat the oven to 220°C/425°F/gas mark 7.

Spread the cauliflower out in a single layer on a baking tray, along with the sliced onion. Add some salt and pepper, the cumin and paprika, pour in the oil, then toss together until well coated. Roast in the preheated oven for 25–30 minutes, until the cauliflower is tender, with just-charred edges, turning everything halfway through the cooking.

Meanwhile, simmer the potatoes in the stock until tender. Add the garlic, chickpeas and lemon zest, simmer for a couple of minutes, then remove from the heat until the cauliflower is ready.

Once the cauliflower is cooked and the onions are golden brown, remove from the oven. Reserve a few small cauliflower florets and a couple of tablespoons of the crispiest onions to garnish, keeping them warm. Add the lemon juice and the rest of the cauliflower to the stock, bring up to a simmer, then blend until smooth.

Taste and add more seasoning, as necessary.

Serve with a swirl of cream, yoghurt or crème fraîche, and top with the reserved roasted onions and cauliflower and a pinch of toasted cumin seeds.

CURRIED PARSNIP

SERVES 2

PREP TIME: 10 MINS · COOK TIME: 35 MINS

WF · GF · DF · V · Ve

2 tablespoons **olive oil**

1 **onion**, diced

1 clove of **garlic**, crushed

500g **parsnips**, about 4 medium parsnips, peeled and chopped into chunks

1 small **eating apple**, peeled, cored and diced

½ teaspoon **ground turmeric**

½ teaspoon **ground coriander**

1 teaspoon **ground cumin**

¼ teaspoon **ground ginger**

¼ teaspoon **fennel seeds**, ground to a powder

4 **cardamom pods**

1 **bay leaf**

750ml **hot vegetable stock**

1 tablespoon **lemon juice**

salt and **freshly ground black pepper**

chilli oil (see page 177), to serve

Because parsnips are naturally rich in sugar, this soup really needs chilli heat to offset its sweetness. If you don't have chilli oil, add a good pinch of chilli flakes or powder to the broth, or a chopped fresh red chilli along with the parsnips.

Place the oil in a large heavy-based saucepan with a lid, set over a medium heat. When hot, add the onion and cook, stirring, for about 10 minutes, until it is translucent. Add the garlic, parsnips, apple, spices and bay leaf and cook for 4 minutes, stirring. Add the stock, bring to a simmer, then cover and cook for 20 minutes, until everything is tender.

Remove from the heat, fish out the bay leaf and cardamom pods, add the lemon juice and blend until smooth. Taste and add seasoning (or chilli, if not using chilli oil). Serve with a swirl of chilli oil on top.

> **\\\\\ TIP /////**
>
> Parsnips also go well with cumin and coriander, so if you like the carrot, cumin & coriander soup on page 12, you can swap in the spices from that recipe, rather than using the Indian-style ones here.

MEERA'S DAILY DAL

SERVES 4

PREP TIME: 10 MINS • COOK TIME: 50 MINS

(**WF** • **GF** if chapattis are omitted) • **V** • (**DF** • **Ve** if yoghurt is omitted)

225g **red lentils**

2 tablespoons **rapeseed oil**

12 **peppercorns** (optional)

4 **cloves** (optional)

1 **onion**, thinly sliced

4 cloves of **garlic**, crushed

6-cm piece of **fresh ginger**, peeled and finely grated

½ teaspoon **chilli powder**

½ teaspoon **ground coriander**

½ teaspoon **ground turmeric**

1 teaspoon **salt**

300g **tinned plum tomatoes**

TO SERVE:

chapattis

yoghurt

Indian pickles

Our friend, food writer Meera Sodha, makes the best dal we know. 'My mum and dad got married in 1975. At the wedding, Dad wore flares, platforms and sideburns, and Mum wore a red sari. They moved to a bedsit in west London with a shared kitchen and a single cupboard. Mum would cook this masoor dal then, and she still cooks it now. This is one of my most treasured recipes: I crave it frequently and never tire of it. It's a foolproof dish, robust and endlessly adaptable, and it yields a result far greater than the effort required to make it.'

In a sieve, rinse the lentils until the water runs clear, then drain and put into a deep, lidded saucepan. Add 600ml of cold water, bring to the boil over a medium to high heat, then cover with the lid and simmer gently for 10–15 minutes without stirring, until thoroughly cooked. Like pasta, lentils will be tender when cooked.

Meanwhile, put the oil into another deep, lidded saucepan on a medium heat. When hot, add the peppercorns and cloves if you're using them. Stir-fry for around a minute, or until you can smell them, then add the onion. Cook for 8–10 minutes, until golden.

Add the garlic and ginger and stir-fry for a further 4 minutes, then add the chilli powder, coriander, turmeric and salt. Stir well, then add the tinned tomatoes. If they're whole, pour them out with one hand and crush them with your other hand to break them up before they hit the pan.

Cover, then turn the heat down and simmer for around 8 minutes. The tomatoes should be looking darker and more paste-like now, with little tomato juice running from them. Add the lentils, using a slotted spoon, then pour in some of their cooking liquid, a little at a time, until you get a good consistency.

Finally, cover the pan with the lid again and cook on a low heat for a further 10 minutes. Taste and adjust the salt, chilli or consistency as you see fit, and serve with chapattis, yoghurt and pickles.

\\\\ TIP ////

Try this with homemade flatbreads (see page 210) or a dollop of raita (see page 171).

MANDY'S LAKSA

SERVES 4

PREP TIME: 15 MINS • COOK TIME: 30 MINS

DF

200g **beansprouts**

200g **long green beans**, ends removed and cut into 3-cm batons

200ml **coconut milk**

1 litre hot **chicken stock**

2 tablespoons **dark brown sugar**

2 tablespoons **tamarind paste**

400g **raw king prawns**

400g **cooked egg noodles**

fresh **mint**, **coriander** or ideally **hot mint**, to serve

FOR THE LAKSA SPICE PASTE:

1 stick of **lemongrass**

65ml **vegetable oil**

½ an **onion**, peeled and roughly chopped

8-cm piece of **fresh ginger**, peeled and roughly chopped

4 cloves of **garlic**, peeled

6 **fresh red chillies**, seeded and roughly chopped

2 teaspoons **salt**

2 teaspoons **ground cumin**

1 tablespoon **ground turmeric**

2 tablespoons **ground coriander**

1 tablespoon **chilli powder**

25g **Thai shrimp paste**

Mandy Yin runs Sambal Shiok, a brilliant Malaysian pop-up restaurant in London. 'Making our signature laksa at the pop-up restaurant is a lengthy, labour-intensive process. This is a simplified version, with a great kick from chilli and shrimp paste (available from Asian supermarkets). It's the perfect winter warmer or for whenever you need a hit of spice.'

Prepare the lemongrass by removing the green top and the hard outer leaves to leave just the white bottom half. Roughly chop the white lemongrass and blend with all the spice paste ingredients in a food processor until you have a smooth, fine paste.

In a medium nonstick saucepan over a low heat, fry the spice paste, continuously stirring for 10–15 minutes until the oil separates.

While the spice paste is cooking, blanch the beansprouts in a saucepan of boiling water for 30 seconds. Remove with a slotted spoon and run under cold water to refresh. Bring the pan of water back to the boil and blanch the green beans for 3 minutes. Again, remove with a slotted spoon and run under cold water to refresh.

Add the coconut milk, chicken stock, brown sugar and tamarind paste to the fried laksa paste in the pan. Heat until boiling, stir and let simmer for a couple of minutes.

Turn the heat up to high and add the raw prawns; cook them for 2 minutes in the broth. Remove with a slotted spoon and set aside. Turn off the heat.

Divide the cooked egg noodles, beansprouts, green beans and cooked prawns between four bowls. Pour the laksa broth on top and garnish with the fresh herbs. Serve immediately.

CONGEE WITH CARAMELIZED SHALLOTS, PEANUTS & RAMEN-STYLE EGGS

SERVES 4

PREP TIME: 15 MINS · COOK TIME: 1½ HOURS

WF · GF · DF

1 litre **hot water**, or hot **chicken** or **vegetable stock**

100g **rice** (any kind of **long-grain rice**)

2-cm piece of **fresh ginger**, peeled and finely sliced

1 clove of **garlic**, peeled and finely sliced

100–200g **cooked chicken** and bones (optional)

2 teaspoons **vegetable oil**

3 **shallots**, thinly sliced

4 **eggs**, at room temperature

TO SERVE:

2 **spring onions**, finely sliced

2 tablespoons **unsalted peanuts**, lightly toasted then roughly crushed

soy sauce

sweet chilli sauce (see page 176)

\\\\ TIP ////
This also works with cooked sliced pork belly, fermented shrimp paste, sautéed Asian mushrooms, grilled fish or cooked chunks of sweet potato.

Congee is a soupy rice porridge served across Asia and China. Congee is its Chinese name, but there are similar dishes in Korea, Thailand, India and beyond. Unlike rice sides, the aim is to cook the rice slowly until it falls apart. We like it with stock, garlic and ginger, topped with crispy fried shallots, crunchy peanuts and ramen-style eggs. A little sweet chilli sauce (see page 176) wouldn't go amiss, too.

Bring the hot water or stock to a simmer in a large pan with a lid. Add the rice, ginger and garlic, plus any chicken and bones. Cover and cook for 1–1½ hours, stirring occasionally. By this time, the rice will have broken down to make a soupy porridge. Add a little water if it's too thick.

Meanwhile, to cook the caramelized shallots, place a pan over a low heat and add the vegetable oil and the sliced shallots. Cook gently for about 15 minutes, stirring often, until deep brown.

Remove any bones from the congee and discard; retrieve any large pieces of chicken and shred, then return to the pan. Keep the congee hot.

Just before serving, cook the eggs. Bring a large pan of salted water to the boil – it should be about 6cm deep. Lower the eggs into the water (chilled eggs may crack) and cook for exactly 6 minutes. Remove from the pan and plunge them into cold water to stop the cooking. When cool enough to handle, peel off the shells, then slice each egg in half, being careful not to lose the runny yolks.

To serve, divide the hot congee between 4 bowls. Place 2 egg halves in each bowl. Top with the spring onions, caramelized shallots, crushed peanuts and a dash of soy sauce and serve with sweet chilli sauce on the side.

\\\ TIP ///

You can use chicken or beef in place of the lamb, or skip the meat altogether.

MOROCCAN LAMB & LENTIL HARIRA

SERVES 4

PREP TIME: 15 MINS • COOK TIME: 3 HOURS 20 MINS

DF

1 tablespoon **olive** or **vegetable oil**

2 **onions**, finely diced

1 stick of **celery**, diced

1 **carrot**, diced

500g **stewing lamb** (we use neck), cut into chunks, ideally with some bone left in

3 cloves of **garlic**, crushed

1½ teaspoons **ground cinnamon**

1½ teaspoons **ground ginger**

1 teaspoon **ground turmeric**

a pinch of **saffron threads**

400g tin of **chopped tomatoes**

1.5 litres **hot water** (or use **chicken stock** if not using bones)

150g **green lentils**, rinsed

75g **uncooked long-grain rice**

400g tin of **chickpeas**, drained (drained weight about 230g)

2 tablespoons **plain flour**

2 tablespoons **lemon juice**

salt and **freshly ground black pepper**

TO SERVE:

fresh coriander leaves, roughly chopped

fresh parsley leaves, roughly chopped

lemon halves

This gently spiced North African soup is traditionally served to break the Ramadan fast, as well as after weddings and at celebrations. Because it contains slowly cooked meat, rice and two kinds of pulse, it is seriously filling.

Place a very large, heavy-based saucepan with a lid over a medium heat. Add the oil, then the onion, celery and carrot and sweat gently for about 10 minutes. Next, turn the heat up and add the lamb. Allow the vegetables to take on a bit of colour while the meat browns, stirring often so nothing burns.

Next, add the garlic, spices and saffron. Stir briefly, then add the tomatoes, the hot water or stock, and plenty of salt and pepper. Cover and bring to a simmer. Skim off any scum that rises to the surface, then cover again. Cook very gently on the hob for 2 hours, or until the meat is tender, then add the lentils. Bring to a fast boil and skim off any scum, then turn down and simmer for a further 45 minutes, or until the lentils are just cooked.

By this point, the lamb should be beginning to fall off the bones (if using bone-in lamb). Lift each chunk from the broth and pull the meat from the bones, then return the meat to the pan, discarding the bones. Add the rice and chickpeas and cook for another 15 minutes.

Whisk together the flour, lemon juice and 4 tablespoons of the hot broth from the pan until smooth, then pour the mixture back into the pan, stirring. Simmer for 5 minutes.

Taste to check the seasoning, adding more salt and pepper if necessary. Serve each bowl garnished with a handful of the chopped fresh herbs and with lemon halves for squeezing over.

BRIGHT & FRESH

GAZPACHO

SERVES 4

PREP TIME: 10 MINS • CHILL TIME: 30 MINS

V · WF · GF · DF · Ve (if Parmesan crunch toasts are omitted)

. . . .

12 **ripe plum tomatoes**, peeled and seeded

2 cloves of **garlic**, crushed to a paste

4 tablespoons very **good-quality extra virgin olive oil**

1½ tablespoons **red wine vinegar**

1 **cucumber** (about 300g), seeded

2 **red peppers**, cored and seeded

2 teaspoons **freshly squeezed lemon juice**

1 **spring onion**, chopped

3–4 **ice cubes**

salt and **freshly ground black pepper**

TO SERVE:

good-quality extra virgin olive oil

1 **spring onion**, very finely chopped

2 tablespoons finely chopped **cucumber**

1 **ripe plum tomato**, peeled seeded and chopped

Parmesan crunch toasts (optional, see page 197)

This chilled soup is thought to come from Andalusia, but versions of it are found in Portugal as well. In truth, its tale might go as far back as the Romans.

If you find raw garlic overpowering, blanch it in boiling water for just 3 minutes, before using.

. . . .

Put the tomatoes into a blender with the garlic, a pinch of salt, the olive oil, vinegar, cucumber, red peppers, lemon juice and spring onion, and blitz just until smooth. Place the soup in the fridge to chill for about 30 minutes before serving – any foam will also disappear. Add the ice cubes to speed up the chilling process; gazpacho should be very, very cold before serving.

Garnish each bowlful with a little more olive oil, spring onion, cucumber and tomatoes, and a grinding of black pepper. Serve with Parmesan crunch toasts.

\ \ \ **TIP** / / /

The oldest gazpacho recipes include a slice of stale bread (crusts removed) soaked in water, added along with the tomatoes before blending, to give the soup a creamier texture. For a fierier version, add a splash of Tabasco. If you love onion, add a chopped shallot to the mix along with the tomatoes. Mix up the garnishes by adding basil, coriander or fresh oregano; or top with guacamole (see page 178), chopped avocado or diced ham.

WATERCRESS SOUP

SERVES 4

PREP TIME: 10 MINS · COOK TIME: 20 MINS

WF · GF · DF · V · (Ve if made with oil)

1 tablespoon **butter** or **olive oil**

2 **onions**, finely diced

200g **white potatoes**, about 2 medium potatoes, peeled and diced

400ml hot **vegetable stock**

400ml **boiling water**

300g **watercress**, plus extra, to serve

1½ teaspoons **lemon juice**

salt and **freshly ground black pepper**

This soup is made, unusually, without cream or crème fraîche, which really lets the peppery watercress flavour come through and keeps its vivid green colour. Stir through 4 tablespoons of cream before serving if you fancy something posher, though.

Place a large pan with a lid over a low heat. Add the butter or oil, onion and a pinch of salt and cook gently until the onion is soft, about 10 minutes. Add the diced potatoes, hot stock and boiling water and simmer until the potatoes are tender.

Meanwhile, place the watercress in a bowl and fill another bowl with cold water. Boil the kettle, then pour the boiling water over the watercress. After no more than a minute, use tongs to remove the watercress and plunge it immediately into the cold water to stop the cooking process. Set aside.

Remove the broth from the heat and pour into a jug blender. Add the blanched watercress and lemon juice, and blitz until absolutely smooth (work in batches if necessary). Taste and adjust the seasoning if necessary. Serve each bowl garnished with a little sprig of watercress.

 **TIP**

About 5 minutes before the potato is cooked, add 100g of frozen peas. Or drop a freshly poached egg into the finished soup before serving; or top with a handful of croutons (see page 196).

SPRING MINESTRONE WITH PESTO

SERVES 4

PREP TIME: 15 MINS • COOK TIME: 10 MINS

V • (DF • Ve if pesto is omitted)

1 tablespoon **olive oil**

2 **spring onions**, finely chopped

3 **shallots**, finely sliced into half moons

150g **broad beans**

150g **long green beans**, trimmed
   if necessary

150g **asparagus**, woody ends removed

800ml hot **homemade vegetable stock**
   (see page 217), **homemade chicken**
   stock (see page 214) or **hot water**

150g **small pasta**, like **macaroni**, broken
   spaghetti or **linguine**

150g **peas**, fresh or frozen

150g **gem** or **romaine lettuce**, shredded

salt and **freshly ground black pepper**

TO SERVE:

fresh chives, chopped

homemade or **fresh pesto** (see page
   186), at room temperature (optional)

\\\\ TIP ////

Meat lovers can add the chicken
meatballs from page 61, or a handful
of frazzled bacon (see page 192).
This is great with a sprinkle of
pangrattato on top (see page 198).

This is the soup for when you need an energy-giving burst of greenery in your life. In spring or summer, swap the seasonal vegetables as you fancy – courgette, fennel, shredded chard, flat beans and spinach are all good. To maximize the vegetables' fresh, green flavours, avoid stock cubes or powder in this soup.

Place the oil in a large heavy-based saucepan with a lid, set over a low heat. When hot, add the spring onions, shallots and a pinch of salt and cook very gently, without browning, until soft, about 10 minutes, stirring often.

Meanwhile prepare the vegetables: blanch the broad beans in boiling water for a couple of minutes, then remove from the heat, drain and cover with cold water. Pop the round little beans out of their leathery shells, discard the shells, and set aside.

Cut the long beans into short lengths of between 5cm and 3cm, without being too uniform about it. Slice off and set aside the asparagus tips, then cut the stems into similarly varying lengths to the beans.

Add the stock or water to the pan, cover and bring to the boil, then tip in the pasta and set a timer for 4 minutes. After this time add, both types of beans, the asparagus and peas, then cover again, bring to the boil and set the timer for 4 minutes. Remove from the heat and check that the pasta is cooked, then stir in the lettuce and some freshly ground black pepper.

Serve straight away, so the vegetables stay lovely and crisp, with a sprinkle of chives and a spoonful of pesto, if using, in each bowl.

UYEN'S VEGAN PHO

SERVES 4 (pictured overleaf)
PREP TIME: 15 MINS • COOK TIME: up to 1 HOUR
WF • GF • DF • V • Ve

FOR THE BROTH:

2 **onions**, peeled, with the ends
  chopped off

2 large pieces of **fresh ginger**, peeled and
  halved lengthways

½ a **mooli**

2 **carrots**, peeled and quartered

1 **fennel bulb**, quartered

2 **celery sticks**, quartered

½ **kolhrabi**, peeled and quartered

10g **rock sugar**

10g **rock salt** (preferably Himalayan pink)

2 **star anise**

1 finger-sized piece of **orange peel**

1 **clove**

1 teaspoon **coriander seeds**

1 teaspoon **fennel seeds**

2 litres **boiling water**

Uyen Luu is one of the best food writers in the UK, and creates beautiful Vietnamese recipes including this one for Vietnam's famous noodle soup, pho (pronounced 'fuh', as in 'duh!'): 'Pho is a favourite breakfast dish among Vietnamese people. The Buddhist sector of the population is vegetarian or vegan at many times throughout the year, but they do not miss out on the seductive power of pho, which wakes the senses for a great start to any day. This recipe can be made with chicken stock, and cooked meat could be added to the bowl. Fish sauce could also be added for a richer umami flavour; you can use any vegetables that are in season or left in the fridge for a nourishing and wholesome meal at any time of the day.'

Ho fun and pho noodles are usually gluten and wheat free. Mooli (sometimes called daikon) is an Asian white radish, and sawtooth is an Asian herb with a strong coriander flavour. These, and rock sugar, are all available in Asian food stores or online.

TO SERVE:

1 tablespoon **flavourless oil**

120g **firm tofu**, sliced into 4 × 1-cm pieces,
  then halved

2 **spring onions**, finely sliced

a handful of **fresh coriander**,
  roughly chopped

4 portions of **fresh ho fun noodles**,
  separated and blanched in boiling
  water, or 400g packet of **dried pho
  noodles** and a dash of **vinegar**

16 **fresh or dried shiitake mushrooms**
  (optional), rehydrated in hot water for
  20 minutes if dried

8 **pak choi leaves**

1 **bird's-eye chilli**, finely sliced

1 **shallot**, finely sliced

salt and **freshly ground black pepper**

GARNISHES:

Thai sweet basil

fresh coriander leaves

bird's eye chillies, sliced

lime wedges

sawtooth (optional)

beansprouts (optional)

sriracha chilli sauce

chilli oil (see page 177)

hoisin sauce (optional)

To make the broth, bring a stove-top griddle pan to a high heat. Char the cut ends of one of the onions along with the ginger and mooli. It will take about 5 minutes on each side to achieve dark caramelized lines.

Put the charred vegetables into a large pan with the rest of the broth ingredients. Cover with a lid and simmer for at least 45 minutes.

Heat the oil in a frying pan over a high heat. Fry the tofu for 5 minutes on each side, until golden brown, then leave to drain on kitchen paper.

Mix together the spring onion and coriander. Remove the carrots from the broth and slice into rounds.

If you are using dried noodles, place them in a pan with a lid, cover with boiling water, add a pinch of salt and the vinegar, and cover with a lid. Leave for 5–10 minutes (or according to the instructions). Drain, rinse in warm water and separate.

Divide the noodles between 4 deep bowls and add a pinch of black pepper. Place 2 slices of tofu, 4 shiitake mushrooms, some sliced carrots from the broth, a couple of pak choi leaves and a little of the chilli in each. Sprinkle with the coriander and spring onion mix and a few slices of raw shallot. Bring the broth to boiling point, then ladle it into the bowls until the noodles are submerged.

Serve with some or all of the suggested garnishes on the side, to add as desired.

JOELLE'S SING-ALONG SOUP

SERVES 4 as a starter, or 2 as a main course
PREP TIME: 5 MINS • COOK TIME: 35 MINS
WF • GF • DF • (V • Ve if made with vegetable stock)

1 tablespoon **olive oil**

½ an **onion**, diced

600g **carrots**, diced

2 cloves of **garlic**, crushed

1 large piece of **fresh ginger**, peeled
    and grated

½ teaspoon **ground cumin**

1 **bay leaf**

500ml good-quality hot **chicken** or
    vegetable stock

salt and **freshly ground black pepper**

chilli oil, to serve (see page 177)

Joelle Davis was John's assistant and now mentors the singers at the singing LEON restaurant in Shaftesbury Avenue. This zingy, singy soup is her creation.

Pour the oil into a large saucepan with a lid, set over a low heat. Add the onion and carrots, cover partially with the lid, and cook gently for about 20 minutes, stirring often, until the onion is translucent. Add the garlic and ginger and cook for 2 minutes, then add the cumin, bay leaf and hot stock. Simmer until the carrots are very tender, about 15 minutes.

Remove from the heat, fish out the bay leaf, and blend until smooth. Taste and add seasoning, if necessary.

Serve drizzled with a little chilli oil.

\\\\ TIP ////
Joelle says that sweating the vegetables for as long as possible is the key to unlocking their flavour.

CHILLED AVOCADO

SERVES 4 as a starter
PREP TIME: 10 MINS
WF · GF · DF · V · Ve

juice of 2 **limes**, or to taste

2 **avocados**, roughly chopped

a pinch of **salt**, to taste

1 teaspoon **hot sauce**, or more to taste

2 **spring onions**, chopped

200g **cucumber**, chopped

300ml **ice-cold water**

TO SERVE:

fresh red chilli, finely chopped

coriander leaves, chopped

2 **tomatoes**, seeded and finely chopped

1 **shallot**, finely diced (optional)

Avocados have become the main currency at LEON, to the extent that they could soon replace the dollar as our reserve currency. Everyone wants to 'av one.

Make this soup as close to serving as possible to preserve its colour.

Squeeze one of the limes into the jug of a blender, and add all the other soup ingredients. Blitz until completely smooth, adding a little more ice-cold water to thin the soup if it seems too thick. Taste and decide if you would like to add the rest of the lime juice, more salt or more hot sauce.

To serve, divide between four bowls and garnish with red chilli, coriander, tomatoes and shallot, if using.

\ \ \ \ TIP / / / ,
Try this served with
tostadas (see page 133).

SHAKSHUKA

SERVES 2

PREP TIME: 10 MINS • COOK TIME: 40 MINS

WF • GF (if bread is omitted) • V (if made with vegetable stock)

2 tablespoons **olive oil**

1 **onion**, diced

1 **red pepper**, cored, seeded and
   roughly diced

4 cloves of **garlic**, crushed

½ teaspoon **ground cumin**

400g tin of **chopped tomatoes**

300ml hot **chicken** or **vegetable stock**

1–2 teaspoons **harissa** (shop-bought or
   see page 173), or 1 teaspoon **sweet** or
   hot paprika

1 teaspoon **soft brown sugar**

2 **eggs**

salt and **freshly ground black pepper**

TO SERVE:

50g **feta** or other **salty crumbly cheese**

a handful of **fresh coriander leaves**,
   roughly chopped

a handful of **fresh parsley leaves**,
   roughly chopped

toasted **bread**, **crusty white rolls** (see
   page 205), toasted **flatbreads** (see
   page 210) or **pitta bread**

Shakshuka is an Israeli breakfast or brunch dish, but has been adopted (and adapted) as part of the worldwide breakfast-for-dinner trend. Making it with a soupier texture means there's more delicious sauce for dipping hunks of bread into. In summer, swap the tinned tomatoes for fresh tomatoes, peeled, seeded and chopped. The harissa isn't essential but its heat makes this a truly hangover-busting shakshuka.

Place the oil in a large, wide heavy-based saucepan with a lid, set over a medium heat. When hot, add a pinch of salt, the onion and red pepper and cook, stirring, for about 10 minutes, until beginning to soften and the onion is translucent. Add the garlic and cook for 1 minute, then add the cumin and cook for a further minute.

Next add the tomatoes, stock and harissa, if using, or paprika. Use a potato masher or the back of a large spoon to crush the lumps of tomato until the sauce is pulpy. Add some black pepper and the sugar, turn the heat down, cover and simmer for 20 minutes.

Break the eggs into the broth, keeping a gap between them, and cover the pan. Cook on a low heat for about 7 minutes, or until the eggs are cooked to your liking. Scoop the eggs and some of the chunky broth out with a ladle and place gently in bowls. Season the top of each egg with more salt and pepper, then scatter over the feta, coriander and parsley. Serve with bread for dipping into the yolks and mopping up the broth.

\\\\ TIP ////

Leave out the feta and top with labneh (see page 183), garlic yoghurt (see page 170), frazzled chorizo (see page 192) or chunks of fried, garlicky sausage.

OLIVER'S BEETROOT WITH CORIANDER, TOFU & BLOOD ORANGE

SERVES 4

PREP TIME: 20 MINS • COOK TIME: 40 MINS

WF • GF • DF • (V • Ve if made with vegetable stock)

2 tablespoons **olive oil**, plus extra for drizzling

2 small **onions**, roughly diced

2 sticks of **celery**, roughly diced

2 large **carrots**, roughly diced

1 teaspoon **coriander seeds**

2 cloves of **garlic**, crushed

6 medium **beetroot**, peeled and chopped

2 **bay leaves**

about 800ml **hot chicken** or **vegetable stock**

juice and zest of 1 **blood orange**

1 teaspoon **sugar**

150g **soft silken tofu**

1-cm piece of **fresh ginger**, peeled and grated

salt and **freshly ground black pepper**

½ a bunch of **fresh coriander**, chopped, to serve

Oliver Rowe is a food stylist and writer, and styled all the good-looking food photographed in this book. This is his beet.

Heat a large saucepan and add the olive oil. Gently fry the onions, celery and carrots with half the coriander seeds until soft and starting to turn golden brown. Add the garlic and cook for a minute.

Add the beetroot to the pan with the bay leaves, cover with stock and simmer until tender but not soft.

While the beetroot is cooking, place the orange juice and sugar in a small saucepan set over a medium heat until slightly thickened and reduced. Blitz the tofu and ginger in a food processor or blender until smooth. Add a little water if needed, to achieve a spooning consistency. Lightly toast the remaining coriander seeds in a hot dry pan and set aside.

When the beetroot is cooked remove the bay leaves, then blend the soup while still warm, until smooth. You may need to add more water or stock to reach the desired consistency. Season to taste.

Before serving, add the orange zest to the soup, then gently bring up to serving temperature. Taste to check the seasoning and add more salt if necessary, then transfer to 4 warm bowls. Swirl a tablespoon of the tofu mix on top of each bowl then drizzle with some olive oil and the orange juice reduction. Sprinkle with the fresh coriander, toasted coriander seeds and some black pepper.

TIP

Serve this with flatbreads (see page 210) or matzo crackers.

TOTALLY SOBA

SERVES 2

PREP TIME: 15 MINS • COOK TIME: 10 MINS

WF • GF (but check noodles) • DF

1 tablespoon **caster sugar**

1 tablespoon **mirin**

1 tablespoon **soy sauce**

1 tablespoon **sake** or **dry sherry** (optional)

2 fillets of sustainably sourced **salmon**

1 heaped tablespoon **dried wakame seaweed** (optional)

125g **soba noodles**

1 tablespoon **vegetable oil**

1 tablespoon **white miso paste**

350ml hot **vegetable** or **homemade fish stock** (see page 216)

150ml **boiling water**

1 head **pak choi**, **bok choy** or other **Asian greens**, trimmed, broken into leaves, large leaves sliced lengthwise

TO SERVE:

2 **spring onions**, finely chopped

2 tablespoons **unsalted roasted peanuts**

fresh **lime juice**

pinch of **black** or **golden sesame seeds**, toasted

pickled ginger (shop-bought, or see page 194)

John spent last October in Tokyo, and one of his favourite restaurant visits was to a soba noodle house near the Hokokuji temple in Kamakura. Japanese soba noodles are made from a non-gluten grass, buckwheat, which gives them a nutty flavour. With this recipe, the key is having everything lined up and ready to go before you start, so the cooked ingredients don't spoil.

First prepare the salmon: mix the sugar, mirin, soy sauce and sake or sherry together, whisking to dissolve the sugar. Place the salmon fillets in this mixture and set aside until ready to cook.

Prepare the broth ingredients: cover the wakame with cold water and set aside to rehydrate for 10–15 minutes. Bring a pan of water to simmering point and add the noodles; cook for 2 minutes, then drain and set aside; keep warm.

Place a frying pan over a medium heat and add the vegetable oil. When hot, lift the salmon out of the marinade and add to the pan. As the salmon cooks its marinade will turn very dark brown. Cook for 1½ minutes or so on each side. Remove from the pan and keep warm. Add the marinade to the frying pan and let it bubble gently for a couple of minutes to reduce while you finish the broth.

Whisk the miso paste, hot stock and boiling water together in the pan you used for the noodles. Bring to a simmer, then add the greens. Once they've wilted, in 30 seconds or so, divide the cooked noodles, broth and greens between 2 bowls.

To serve, scatter over the spring onions and peanuts. Drizzle the warm salmon with a little of the reduced teriyaki sauce from the pan, then place on top of the soup. Squeeze a little lime juice over the whole lot, sprinkle over a pinch of toasted sesame seeds and serve with the pickled ginger on the side.

\\\\ TIP ////

While naturally gluten-free, some
of the flour used in soba noodles is
milled by machinery that also mills
gluten-containing products, and
still others contain wheat flour, so
check the packet to be sure. Soba
noodles, miso paste, mirin and
pickled ginger are available in large
supermarkets; wakame is available
online or in Japanese stores.

INDIAN KADHI YOGHURT

SERVES 4 with rice and other curry dishes
PREP TIME: 5 MINS • COOK TIME: 15 MINS
WF • GF • V

250g **Greek-style yoghurt** (choose something tangy)
1 heaped tablespoon **gram flour**
½ teaspoon **grated fresh ginger**
½ teaspoon **ground turmeric**
¼ teaspoon **chilli powder**
500ml **cold water**
salt

FOR TEMPERING:
2 tablespoons **vegetable oil**
1 teaspoon **mustard seeds**
½ teaspoon **cumin seeds**
lots of **freshly ground black pepper**
10 **curry leaves**
2 teaspoons **finely chopped fresh green chilli**
pinch of **salt**

TO SERVE:
fresh coriander leaves
steamed **rice**

This sour, hot yoghurt soup gets its spicy flavour from the fried and tempered spices that are poured over before serving. It leaves you feeling good-tempered and spicy.

Put the yoghurt into a large bowl and sift in the gram flour. Add the grated ginger, turmeric, chilli powder and a generous pinch of salt and whisk until absolutely smooth. Add the water and whisk again.

Place a saucepan over a low heat and add the yoghurt mixture. Warm it slowly, stirring, so that the yoghurt doesn't split, bringing it eventually to a low simmer. (It will look and taste fairly unexciting at this point; don't worry.) Simmer for 5 minutes, still stirring, otherwise lumps will form on the bottom, and allow to thicken until soupy. Remove from the heat.

Divide the soup between 4 serving bowls. Just before serving, pour the oil into a small pan set over a medium heat. Add the mustard seeds, cumin seeds, black pepper, curry leaves, chilli and salt and cook for a minute or two, until the seeds start to pop and the leaves frazzle. Remove from the heat and spoon the tempered spices over the soup. Finish with a few fresh coriander leaves and serve straight away, with steamed rice.

＼＼＼ TIP ／／／

Adding the gram flour stabilizes the yoghurt so it can be cooked – it's available in large supermarkets and Asian food stores. As well as being used in all sorts of Indian and gluten-free breads and pastries, gram flour also makes terrific chocolate brownies. For a crunchier topping, add a handful of nutty dukkah (see page 190).

PERKY PEA & MINT

SERVES 4 as a starter, or 2 as a hearty lunch
PREP TIME: 10 MINS • COOK TIME: 10 MINS
WF • GF

a knob of **butter** or 1 tablespoon
   cooking oil
2 **spring onions**, chopped
50–60g **smoked bacon** or **ham** (about
   2 rashers), roughly chopped (optional)
250ml hot **chicken** or **vegetable stock**
250ml **boiling water**
500g **peas**, fresh or frozen
1–2 teaspoons freshly squeezed
   lemon juice
salt and **freshly ground black pepper**

TO SERVE:
2–4 tablespoons **single cream** or **soured
   cream** (optional)
finely chopped fresh mint

This soup feels like spring, even if made with frozen peas in the depths of winter. Using half water, half stock means the pea flavour isn't overwhelmed. It was a big hit in the early days of LEON. We may be inspired to bring it back.

Set a pan over a low heat and add the butter or oil. Gently sauté the spring onions and the bacon or ham, if using, for 5 minutes, but don't allow to brown. Add the hot stock and boiling water, then the peas, and bring to the boil. Simmer for a couple of minutes, or slightly longer if using fresh peas, then blend until smooth.

Add a little black pepper and 1 teaspoon of lemon juice, then taste to see if the soup needs salt, which will depend on whether you used bacon and how salty it is. Add the rest of the lemon juice, or more, if necessary.

Serve garnished with a swirl of cream or soured cream, if using, and the finely chopped mint.

\\\\ TIP ////
Swap the mint for basil, or try yoghurt instead of cream. A little extra crispy bacon or some cured ham, like prosciutto, is lovely on top, as is freshly grated Parmesan.

MEXICAN-STYLE CORN & RED PEPPER WITH GUACAMOLE

SERVES 4

PREP TIME: 10 MINS • COOK TIME: 30 MINS

(**WF** • **GF** but check tostadas) • **V** • (**DF** • **Ve** if cheese and cream are omitted)

2 tablespoons **olive oil**

1 **onion**, diced

1 stick of **celery**, diced

1 **red pepper**, cored, seeded and diced

1 tablespoon finely chopped seeded **red chilli**, plus extra to garnish if liked

2 cloves of **garlic**, crushed

1½ teaspoons **ground cumin**

1½ teaspoons **ground coriander**

1 litre hot **vegetable stock**

1 **bay leaf**

350g **sweetcorn**, fresh or frozen (not tinned)

freshly squeezed **lime juice**, to taste

salt and **freshly ground black pepper**

TO SERVE:

feta, **soured cream** or **Mexican queso fresco** (optional)

homemade **guacamole**, at room temperature (see page 178)

coriander leaves

tostadas (see tip)

Chilli heads will love this with smoked chilli flakes, chipotle sauce or hot smoked paprika added along with the other spices.

Place a large saucepan over a medium heat. Add the oil, onion, celery, a pinch of salt and pepper and cook gently, stirring often, for 10 minutes. Next add the red pepper and chilli and cook for 5 minutes. Then add the garlic, ground cumin and ground coriander and cook for a couple of minutes, stirring again.

Add the stock and bay leaf and bring to a simmer. If using fresh corn, add it now. Simmer for 10 minutes, or until the vegetables are tender. If using frozen corn, add it once the other vegetables are tender, bring back to the boil, then cook for 3 minutes.

Remove from the heat, fish out the bay leaf and blend the soup until smooth. If it seems a little thin, return to the heat and reduce for a few minutes.

Remove from the heat again. Taste and add a tablespoon of lime juice, then taste again and add more lime, salt or pepper, as necessary. (Remember that feta is salty, if you are serving it with the soup.)

Serve each bowl with soured cream or cheese, if using, plus a dollop of guacamole, some more chopped red chilli and a few coriander leaves, with some crunchy tostadas on the side.

> ### ⟍⟍⟍ TIP ⁄⁄⁄
>
> Crispy tortilla tostadas are like edible spoons. To make them, heat the oven to 200°C/400°F/gas mark 6. Mix a pinch of salt with a couple of tablespoons of flavourless oil (and some smoked paprika or chilli powder if liked), then brush the mix over 4 small corn tortillas. Cook in the oven for 4 minutes, then turn and cook for 2 minutes until crisp.

POSH

OLIVER'S JERUSALEM ARTICHOKE SOUP WITH ROAST OLIVES & GOATS' CHEESE

SERVES 4

PREP TIME: 20 MINS • COOK TIME: 50 MINS

V

2 or 3 slices of **sourdough bread**

4 tablespoons **olive oil**, plus extra
for drizzling (optional)

12 good-quality **green** or **black olives**,
with stones in

2 **onions**, diced

3 sticks of **celery**, diced

2 fresh **bay leaves**

1 sprig of **fresh thyme**

2–3 cloves of **garlic**, peeled and chopped

500g **Jerusalem artichokes**

about 800ml hot **vegetable stock** or
hot water

200ml **milk** (optional)

salt and **freshly ground black pepper**

50g crumbly **goats' cheese**, **crème
fraîche** or **yoghurt**, to serve

> ### \\\\ TIP ////
>
> A little bit of good balsamic,
> pomegranate molasses, chilli
> flakes, paprika, toasted ground
> cumin, black onion seed or toasted
> crushed walnuts could all be
> sprinkled or drizzled over the top.

Oliver Rowe can make any bowl of tucker look pretty. (Look out for his memoir-cookbook, **Food For All Seasons.***)*

Heat the oven to 180°C/350°F/gas mark 4. Pick the bread into large irregular crumbs, the size of a pea, and toss in a bowl with a tablespoon of the oil and a pinch of salt. Spread out on a baking tray and roast until golden brown, about 8–10 minutes.

Stone the olives – don't worry if the flesh gets torn as you go – and toss with another tablespoon of oil. Spread out on another baking tray and roast for about 25 minutes. Leave to cool on kitchen paper.

Heat the remaining olive oil in a medium saucepan, then add the onions, celery, bay leaves, thyme and a good pinch of salt, to help soften the vegetables. Cook gently for 5 minutes or so, then add the garlic and cook until light golden brown.

As the other vegetables cook, clean and roughly chop the Jerusalem artichokes. They often have grit stuck in their nooks and crannies, so soak them a bit first and scrub them carefully. You can peel them, but I prefer not to, as you lose some of the earthy flavour. Add them to the vegetables in the pan. Cook for a few minutes, then cover with the stock or water and bring to a gentle simmer. Cook until the artichokes are very tender, about 20 minutes.

Remove from the heat, fish out the bay leaves, and blitz in a blender until smooth. If you want, you can thin the soup a bit at this point with some more stock, water or the milk. Taste and season well. If you want your soup to be really smooth, you can pass it through a sieve, using the back of a ladle to help it on its way.

To serve, divide the soup between 4 bowls, drizzle with good olive oil if liked, crumble the cheese over the top and sprinkle with the breadcrumbs and roasted olives.

ASPARAGUS WITH ROMESCO

SERVES 4 as a starter, or 2 as a main course
PREP TIME: 10 MINS · COOK TIME: 20 MINS
(**WF · GF** if romesco sauce is omitted) · **V** (if made with vegetable stock) · (**DF · Ve** if olive oil used)

1 tablespoon **butter** or **olive oil**

3 **spring onions**, finely chopped

550g **asparagus**, woody ends removed

500ml hot **chicken** or **vegetable stock**

1 teaspoon **lemon juice**

salt and **freshly ground black pepper**

2 heaped tablespoons **romesco sauce**,
(shop-bought or see page 188), at room
temperature, to serve

It makes us a bit sad to see skinny, limp asparagus on sale in December, when we grow delicious, chubby stalks in the UK and Europe during summer. This is a soup best made when local asparagus is in season, rather than freighted halfway around the world.

Place a large deep pan over a low to medium heat and add the butter or oil. When hot, add the spring onions and a good pinch of salt. Cook gently, stirring, until soft but not brown.

Slice the asparagus into short lengths, separating the tips from the main stalks. Slice 4 of the tips lengthwise and blanch briefly in a pan of boiling water, then set aside for garnish.

Add the stock to the pan, turn up the heat, bring to a simmer, then add the stalks and cook for 2 minutes. Next, add the tips and cook for a further 3 minutes, just until the asparagus is tender, but still a vivid green. Remove from the heat and stir in the lemon juice along with a good grinding of black pepper.

Blend the soup until smooth, in batches if necessary. Taste and add more salt, pepper or lemon juice, as necessary. Divide between warmed bowls and top with a spoonful of the romesco sauce and the reserved asparagus.

\\\\ TIP ////

Some recipes for asparagus soup suggest boiling the poor stuff for 30 minutes or more. This also makes us sad, as well as making the soup a sort of muddy taupe colour. Asparagus needs just the briefest of cooks, so keep it short and sweet.

FRENCH ONION

SERVES 4 as a starter, or 2–3 as a hearty main course
PREP TIME: 15 MINS • COOK TIME: up to 2 HOURS 40 MINS

1 heaped tablespoon **salted butter**

1 tablespoon **olive oil**

1kg **onions**, about 5 onions, finely sliced

1 teaspoon **sugar**

1.5 litres good-quality, hot **beef stock** (see page 215)

2 tablespoons **brandy**

2 or 3 slices of **baguette** per person, depending on bowl shape

100–150g **Gruyère**, grated

salt and **freshly ground black pepper**

chives, chopped, to serve

Although this posh classic takes a while to make, it's the kind of thing you can leave to bubble away while you get on with cooking other things, so it's a perfect starter for a swanky supper. It can be made in advance and reheated, but cook the toasted cheese tops just before serving.

Making this bistro stalwart might make you cry but it's worth it. For speed, slice the onions on a mandolin, or shred them in an electric chopper or food processor.

Set a large, wide, heavy-based pan with a lid over a medium heat. Add the butter and oil and when foaming, tip in the sliced onions along with the sugar. Stir to coat the onions in the fat, then cook, stirring often, for about 15 minutes, or until the onions just begin to colour.

Turn the heat right down and cook very gently, stirring often to stop the onions sticking, for 45 minutes–1½ hours, depending on your pan. This step can't be rushed – you want the onions to slowly caramelize and darken to a deep golden brown, and if the heat is too high they will burn and the soup will taste bitter.

Once the onions are a lovely, even brown in colour, season generously with salt and freshly ground pepper.

Next, add the hot stock, scraping up any stuck-on onion bits from the bottom of the pan. Bring the broth up to a simmer and cook as gently as possible for 45 minutes. Add the brandy and cook for a further 15 minutes. Taste and add more seasoning, if necessary.

To serve, you will need enough sliced baguette to almost cover each bowl of soup. Heat the grill and toast the baguette slices.

If you have ovenproof soup bowls, assemble by topping each bowl of soup with slices of toast and some grated cheese, and placing under the hot grill to melt the cheese.

If not, warm up your serving bowls. Place the toasts on a baking tray and cover each with a generous layer of the Gruyère. Grill until the cheese is oozing and bubbling; 3 or 4 minutes. Fill each bowl with hot soup and top with the cheese-covered toasts. Garnish with chives and allow the cheese and bread to slowly sink into the soup with each bite.

\ \ \ \ **TIP** / / / ,

Rub the bread with garlic
after toasting, if you like.

MUSHROOM SOUP

SERVES 2

PREP TIME: 10 MINS • COOK TIME: 30 MINS

(**WF** • **GF** if toast is omitted) • **V** (if made with vegetable stock)

1 tablespoon **olive oil**

a knob of **butter**

1 **onion**, finely chopped

2 cloves of **garlic**, sliced

1 teaspoon **thyme leaves**

6 sprigs of **fresh flat-leaf parsley**, leaves picked and finely chopped, stems reserved and roughly chopped

300g **mixed mushrooms**, sliced

500ml hot **chicken** or **vegetable stock**

4 tablespoons **single cream**

zest of ½ a **lemon**

salt and **freshly ground black pepper**

TO SERVE:

buttered toast

extra virgin olive oil

An earthy, creamy soup.

Place a large pan over a medium heat and add the oil and butter. When melted together add the onion and a pinch of salt and cook gently for about 8 minutes, stirring and without colouring the onion. Next, add the garlic and cook for 1 minute, then add the thyme, parsley stems and mushrooms and cook until browned (don't worry if the onion browns a little at this point too). Once nicely golden, remove a couple of tablespoons of mushrooms and reserve for the garnish; keep warm.

Add the stock to the pan along with a good grinding of black pepper. Bring up to a simmer, then cover and leave to cook for 10–15 minutes.

To serve, remove from the heat, add the cream and lemon zest, then blend until smooth. Taste and add more seasoning if necessary – how much salt you will need will depend on your stock.

Serve the creamy soup with hot buttered toast, something tangy and crunchy like sourdough. Garnish with the reserved mushrooms, a drizzle of extra virgin olive oil and the chopped fresh parsley.

\ \ \ TIP / / /

Garnish this soup with chives, spritz with truffle oil, or even shave over a little fresh truffle if you have some lying around. Go retro and add a splash of sherry or even brandy along with the cream, and a bit of freshly grated nutmeg.

DON'T TAKE THE BISQUE

SERVES 4 (pictured overleaf)

PREP TIME: 20 MINS · COOK TIME: 1½ HOURS

WF · GF

- 2 **cooked** or **live lobsters**, about 600g each
- 4 tablespoons **olive oil**
- 2 knobs of **butter**
- 2 **onions**, diced
- 2 **carrots**, diced
- 2 sticks of **celery**, diced
- 2 cloves of **garlic**, crushed
- 1 tablespoon **tomato purée**
- 1 sprig of **fresh tarragon**, leaves only
- 1 **bay leaf**
- 200ml **white wine**
- 3 tablespoons **dry sherry**
- 1 litre good quality hot **fresh fish** or **shellfish stock** (not from a cube, see page 216), or a mixture of stock and poaching liquid if using fresh lobsters
- 2½ tablespoons **rice flour**
- 2 tablespoons **thick double cream**, plus extra to serve
- ¼ teaspoon **cayenne pepper**, or more to taste (optional)
- 1 teaspoon **lemon juice**
- **salt** and **freshly ground black pepper**
- **toast**, to serve

If you really want to show off, this is the soup for you. This version is easy-ish while still being a bit over the top and luxurious.

You can use this recipe with crab too. If you don't have fresh fish stock, use chicken stock instead, or homemade vegetable stock, but not vegetable or fish stock from a cube or powder.

Kill and cook the lobsters, if using live ones. (See tip opposite for how to do this fairly humanely.) Retain any liquid from the cooking process.

Split the cooked lobsters open, using a sharp knife or kitchen shears. Remove the sweet white meat from the shell and claws and set aside. Scrape out the greenish gunk from inside and remove the slightly frilly gills, and discard. Keep the shells and any red roe, as these will add flavour to the soup. If you can't get the mouth parts completely clean, discard these too. Chop the shells into chunks small enough to fit into your pan.

Put the oil and 1 knob of butter into a large pan with a lid, set it over a fairly high heat, and when hot, add the lobster shells. Sauté until beginning to brown, 6–8 minutes.

Next, turn the heat down to low. Add the onion, carrot and celery and sweat for 8 minutes, without browning. Add the garlic and tomato purée, and cook, stirring, for 2 minutes. Turn the heat up again, add the tarragon, bay leaf, white wine and sherry, and cook for 3 or 4 minutes, letting the wine bubble merrily. Then add the stock, or stock and poaching liquid if you started with live lobsters. Bring to a gentle simmer, cover and cook for an hour.

Strain the broth into a clean pan through a sieve. Separate the shells from the vegetables and pick out any little bits of meat still clinging to them. Squeeze the juices from the claws through the sieve too, pressing the shells with the back of a wooden spoon to get all the flavour out. Return the vegetables and any bits of meat to the pan, picking them over beforehand to avoid any large bits of shell.

Sift the rice flour into the cream and whisk until smooth. Add one-third of the reserved lobster tail and claw meat to the broth, along with the cream mixture, and gently bring to a simmer again, stirring, until the broth thickens, about 5 minutes. Working in batches if necessary, blend until completely smooth (a jug blender tends to be more effective for this particular soup). If your blender won't get the soup completely smooth, sieve it again. Taste and add the cayenne pepper, if using, and the lemon juice, along with more seasoning if necessary.

Chop the remaining reserved lobster meat into bite-sized pieces. Melt the remaining knob of butter in a small frying pan over a medium heat and, once melted, add the lobster pieces. Heat through gently. Divide the soup between small bowls and garnish with the hot lobster meat and a little extra cream.

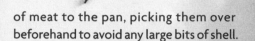

\\\\ TIP ////

If using live lobsters or crabs, be sure to kill them as humanely as possible first – don't throw them into hot water still alive. First, stun each lobster by popping it into the freezer for an hour or so, then quickly kill it by pressing a sharp knife or skewer through the cross on the back of the lobster's head. For crabs, turn them over, lift up the triangular flap on the abdomen, and pierce there with a skewer. Cook straight away.

\\\\| TIP |///

Instead of a smooth soup, don't
blend and either add shredded white
cabbage and cooked kidney beans
along with the garlic for the last
few minutes of cooking, or omit the
vinegar and add 4 tablespoonfuls
of sauerkraut instead. Top with
crumbled feta or mild goats' cheese,
instead of soured cream.

BORSCHT –
THE SOUP THAT CAN'T BE BEET

SERVES 4
PREP TIME: 15 MINS · COOK TIME: 30 MINS
WF · GF · V (if made with vegetable stock)

a knob of **butter**

1 teaspoon **vegetable oil**

350g **beetroot**, peeled and chopped

1 small **onion**, chopped

1 small **leek**, white part only, chopped

1 stick of **celery**, chopped

150g **potato**, 1 medium potato, peeled
and diced

1 litre hot **beef** or **vegetable stock**

a pinch of **allspice**

1 **bay leaf**

1 clove of **garlic**, crushed, or more if you
love garlic

½ tablespoon **cider vinegar**

½ tablespoon **lemon juice**

freshly ground black pepper

TO SERVE:

soured cream

sprigs of **fresh dill**

Borscht is often served as a chunky soup, but we love it when it's smooth and earthy, with the tang of soured cream to cut through the sweet beets. It's another soup for which there are hundreds of different recipes – there are beetroot soups made right across northern and eastern Europe and into Russia, so feel free to play around with the recipe.

Your wooden spoons may never come back from cooking this vivid dish. Wear gloves to prevent your hands from turning pink if you have any job interviews coming up.

Melt the butter with the oil in a large pan over a low heat. Add the beetroot, onion, leek and celery and sweat for 10 minutes or so, stirring often so that the vegetables don't catch on the bottom. Add the potato to the pan, then add the hot stock, allspice, bay leaf and some black pepper. Bring up to a simmer, then leave to cook for 15–20 minutes, or until all the vegetables are really tender. For the last 5 minutes of cooking, add the crushed garlic.

Remove from the heat, fish out the bay leaf and stir in the vinegar and lemon juice. Taste and add more seasoning, if necessary.

Blend the soup until smooth. Serve with a tablespoon of soured cream swirled into each bowl, topped with fresh dill.

ALL ABOUT THAT BOUILLABAISSE

SERVES 4 (pictured overleaf)
PREP TIME: 45 MINS · COOK TIME: 35 MINS

FOR THE ROUILLE:

1 or 2 cloves of **garlic**, green stem
removed if necessary, crushed to
a paste

2 **roasted red peppers** (see method on
page 34, or from a jar, drained)
or 4 tablespoons shop-bought
roasted pepper paste

1 slice of **slightly stale white bread**,
crusts removed, torn into pieces

3 tablespoons **cold water**

a pinch of **saffron strands**

1 **egg yolk**

¼ teaspoon **cayenne pepper** (optional)

175ml **olive oil**, with a light flavour

1 teaspoon **lemon juice**, or to taste

salt and **freshly ground black pepper**

FOR THE BOUILLABAISSE:

3 tablespoons **olive oil**

1 **leek**, finely chopped

1 **onion**, finely chopped

1 **fennel bulb**, cored and finely sliced, the
green fronds chopped and reserved

6 cloves of **garlic**, crushed

200g tinned **chopped plum tomatoes**,
drained

When made in Marseille by French fishermen, this soup-stew involves separating the cooked fish and potatoes from the broth, removing them in the order they cook, and serving the soup as a starter and the cooked fish as a second course. We cheat and – sacrilegiously – make it in a different order, which is a lot easier and still delicious, but results in a lighter broth.

If you can find rascasse fish, they, along with sea robin (grondin) and conger, are part of the traditional recipe – although even fishermen admit that they use what they catch.

To make the rouille: place everything except the oil and lemon juice in a blender or food processor and blitz until completely smooth. With the motor running, add the oil in a steady stream, so that it emulsifies and forms a smooth, thick sauce. Taste and add the lemon juice, if necessary, plus more salt, pepper or cayenne, if liked.

To make the soup: use the biggest pan with a lid that you have. Pour in the oil, set it over a medium heat and add the leek, onion and fennel. Sweat gently for 10 minutes, then add the garlic and drained tomatoes and cook, stirring, for a couple of minutes. Next add the herbs and the potatoes.

Season really well, then mix everything in the pan together. Place the fish pieces in a single layer on top. Add the saffron to the stock, then pour this mixture over the fish and vegetables, along with the pastis. Don't stir. Turn up the heat and bring to a fast boil. As soon as the fish is cooked, remove from the pan with tongs and set aside, but don't worry if some small pieces remain – they will fall apart and add flavour and texture to the soup.

BOUILLABAISSE CONTINUED:

6 whole sprigs of **fresh parsley**

1 **bay leaf**

3 sprigs of **fresh thyme**

300g **waxy potatoes**, about 3 medium potatoes, peeled and sliced into ½-cm pieces

600g firm **fish fillets**, cut into chunks: any mixture of **hake**, **bream**, **turbot**, **mullet**, **gurnard**, **cod**, **bass**, **monkfish** and ideally including **rascasse**, but you can include whichever sustainably sourced fish you can find

a generous pinch of **saffron threads**

800ml good-quality hot **fresh fish** or **shellfish stock** (not from a cube, see page 216), or **chicken stock** (see page 214) if you can't get fresh fish stock

175ml **pastis**, **Pernod** or other anise-flavoured liqueur

600g **mixed shellfish** and **crustaceans**, any mixture of small **crabs**, **mussels**, **clams**, **raw shell-on prawns**

salt and **freshly ground black pepper**

12 large **garlicky croutons**, made from a baguette, to serve (see page 196)

Continue cooking the broth at a fast boil for 5 minutes (this helps to emulsify the fat and gelatin from the fish into the broth) then turn down the heat and cook until the potatoes are just done. Taste and add more seasoning to the broth if necessary.

If you're adding small crabs to the soup, do so now – but kill them first (see note on page 145), otherwise they will shed their legs and potentially stomach contents into the soup. Cook for 10 minutes, at a high simmer, covered, then add the rest of the seafood and the cooked fish pieces and cook for 3 minutes, covered again.

Discard any clams or mussels which haven't opened during cooking. Prawns should be pink all the way through.

There are two ways to serve this dish: either place a couple of crisp, garlicky croutons in the bottom of each of 4 wide soup bowls. Spread each with a spoonful of the rouille, then ladle the soup, fish and seafood on top, allowing the bread and rouille to melt into the broth.

Alternatively, spread 2 croutons per person with rouille and serve on top of the soup. Sprinkle the reserved fennel fronds over the soup. Serve the remaining rouille and croutons on the side, plus bowls for shells and plenty of napkins.

\\\ TIP ///

Apart from strong-flavoured oily fish like mackerel, most fish are suitable for bouillabaisse, including squid – just adjust the cooking time to suit each type of seafood: cleaned raw squid rings need only a minute cooking in the pan, whereas meatier fish like monkfish will need 4 or 5 minutes.

LOHIKIETTO

SERVES 2

PREP TIME: 10 MINS · COOK TIME: 20 MINS

WF · GF (if rye bread is omitted)

. . . .

2 knobs of **butter**

1 **onion**, finely diced

300g **waxy potatoes**, about 3 medium
potatoes, peeled and cut into small
pieces

600ml hot **fresh fish stock** (see page 216),
or hot **chicken** or **vegetable stock**

1 **bay leaf**

a tiny pinch of **allspice**

300g sustainably sourced **salmon fillet**,
skinned and cut into 3-cm cubes

2 tablespoons **finely chopped fresh dill**

4 tablespoons **double cream**

salt and **freshly ground black pepper**

buttered rye bread, to serve (see
page 206)

This Finnish salmon, dill, allspice and potato broth adds up to way more than the sum of its parts – it's really full of flavour, and easy to see why it's such a favourite in salmon-rich Finland. Get sustainably sourced salmon and if possible, use fresh fish stock. If you can't, use a chicken or vegetable stock cube instead, rather than a fish stock cube.

. . . .

Place 1 knob of the butter in a heavy-based saucepan with a lid, set over a low heat. When foaming, add the onion and a pinch of salt and cook gently, stirring, until the onion is just translucent. Don't allow to brown. Add the potatoes, stock, some black pepper, the bay leaf and a tiny pinch of allspice – its flavour is fairly strong, so go easy, as you can always add more later if you want to. Bring up to a simmer, cover, and cook until the potatoes are tender, about 15 minutes. Remove the bay leaf.

Add the salmon and half the dill and simmer until the salmon is just cooked. Remove from the heat and gently stir in the cream and the remaining knob of butter.

Serve garnished with the rest of the fresh dill with slices of buttered rye bread on the side.

⟍⟍\\ TIP //⟋⟋

Stocks of salmon in the sea are
running low. Choose river salmon or
sustainable, organically farmed fish.

SWEET SOUPS

CHILLED CHERRY SOUP

SERVES 4–6 as a starter or dessert

PREP TIME: 5 MINS • CHILL TIME: 1 HOUR • COOK TIME: 20 MINS

WF · GF · V

350g **sour** or **sweet cherries** (the stones can be left in for extra flavour), fresh or frozen

500ml **boiling water**

½ a **cinnamon stick**

2 **cloves**

2 × 5-cm strips of **lemon zest**, cut with a peeler

50g **soft brown sugar**

300ml **full-fat soured cream**

2–6 teaspoons **lemon juice**, or more, to taste

The Hungarian version of this soup, **meggyleves**, *is the best known, but there are similar cherry soups served across eastern Europe as starters. In France they are served as desserts with ice cream. Traditionally this is made with sour Morello cherries, cooked with the stones in. If using sour cherries, you may need a little more sugar. But it is not mandate-cherry.*

Put the cherries, water, cinnamon, cloves, lemon zest and sugar into a large pan with a lid. Cover and bring to a simmer, then cook for 10 minutes if using fresh cherries, or 15 minutes if using frozen, until the cherries have started to lose their shape.

Remove from the heat. Place the soured cream in a bowl and add a ladleful of the hot soup, then whisk to combine and temper the cream. Then add another ladleful and do the same again. This prevents the cream from curdling. When smooth, pour back into the pan and combine with the rest of the soup.

Return to a very low heat and cook for a further 5 minutes; do not boil. Add the lemon juice gradually, to taste – the soup should be both sweet and tart, and how much you need depends on your cherries.

Remove from the heat and leave to cool. Once cooled, put into the fridge and chill for an hour.

When ready to serve, remove the cinnamon, cloves, lemon zest and cherry stones (if left in at the beginning).

\\\ TIP ///

Use full-fat soured cream as low-fat versions are less stable when heated, and may curdle in the saucepan even if tempered.

ANYONE FOR TENNIS?

SERVES 4 as a starter or dessert
PREP TIME: 5 MINS · CHILL TIME: 1 HOUR
WF · GF · DF · V · Ve

350g **ripe strawberries**, hulled, plus
   1 extra **strawberry**, finely sliced,
   to garnish
250g **cucumber**, peeled and seeded,
   plus 8 thin slices to garnish
freshly squeezed **lime juice**, to taste
maple syrup or **caster sugar**, to taste
fine salt, to taste

This soup is Wimbledon in a bowl – summer freshness. The bright flavours of strawberry and cucumber bring out the best in each other.

Roughly chop the strawberries and cucumber and place in a blender. Blitz to a smooth purée.

The quantity needed of the rest of the ingredients depends on how sweet and ripe the strawberries are. Taste first, and add the remaining flavours gradually, a pinch or dash at a time – you may not need the maple syrup or sugar at all.

Chill in the fridge for an hour before serving, then taste and season or sweeten again if necessary, as the flavours will flatten out when cold. Serve in small bowls, garnished with the sliced cucumber and strawberry, as a starter, palate cleanser or light dessert.

\\\ TIP ///
A dollop of soured cream, crème fraîche, yoghurt or even vanilla ice cream works brilliantly here if serving as pudding. Add the leaves from a sprig of mint or basil to the blender for a more fragrant version of the soup.

CHOCOLATE SOUP WITH SWEET & SALTY BRIOCHE CROUTONS

SERVES 4
PREP TIME: 5 MINS • COOK TIME: 10 MINS
V

FOR THE BRIOCHE CROUTONS:

50g **brioche**, crusts removed, cut into
    1-cm dice
a pinch of **flaky sea salt**

FOR THE CHOCOLATE SOUP:

200ml **double cream**
1½ tablespoons **milk**
150g good-quality **dark eating chocolate**,
    at least 70% cocoa solids, broken
    into pieces
2 tablespoons **strong black coffee**
1 tablespoon **Grand Marnier** (optional)

Rebecca loves this soup to a pretty ridiculous degree. It's incredibly rich, so serve it in small portions. It's very quick to cook and is best served warm, so make it at the last minute. P.S. John loves it too.

Heat the oven to 180°C/350°F/gas mark 4. Toss the diced brioche in the salt, then spread it in a single layer on a baking tray and place in the oven for 10 minutes, or until crisp and golden. Remove and keep warm.

To make the soup, put the cream into a pan and bring to just below the boil, then remove from the heat. Add the milk, then the broken chocolate, whisking until the chocolate has melted into the cream and the soup is silky smooth. Pour in the coffee and Grand Marnier, if using. Divide between 4 very small bowls, glasses (check the soup is warm rather than hot if using glass), ramekins or mugs and top with the warm brioche croutons. Serve immediately.

\\\\\ TIP /////

This is a perfect summer
dessert with a scoop of fruity
sorbet melting on top.

CHILLED MELON

SERVES 4 as a palate cleanser or dessert
PREP TIME: 5 MINS • CHILL TIME: 1 HOUR
WF • GF • DF • V • Ve

1 very ripe **cantaloupe melon**, peeled, seeded and chopped into chunks

2 tablespoons **apple juice** or **water**, or more, to achieve your desired consistency

a small pinch of **salt**

fresh basil, sliced into thin strips, to serve

Only really ripe melons will do for this fruit soup — because it is chilled you need all the natural sweetness you can get.

Blitz the melon in a blender until completely smooth. If really thick, add a couple of tablespoons of apple juice or water to loosen, but not too much, as it dilutes the melon's flavour. Add the salt, then chill the soup for an hour before serving.

Serve in small bowls or glasses with the basil on top.

CARDAMOM-SPICED ROASTED PEACH

SERVES 4 as a starter, palate cleanser or dessert
PREP TIME: 10 MINS · COOK TIME: 15 MINS · CHILL TIME: 2 HOURS
WF · GF · DF · V

6 **ripe peaches**, stones removed, cut
　　into chunks
½ teaspoon **ground cardamom** or seeds
　　from 8 **cardamom pods**, ground to
　　a powder
2 tablespoons **runny honey**
2 tablespoons **soft brown sugar**
100–250ml **cold water**
1 teaspoon **lime juice**
salt
fresh mint leaves, to garnish

We imagine we would enjoy this sitting at a small table in a Middle Eastern rose garden. Meanwhile, we are enjoying it in Peckham. Roasting the peaches with cardamom makes them fragrant and spicy.

Heat the oven to 220°C/425°F/gas mark 7. Line a baking tray with foil, then add the peaches, cardamom, honey and sugar and toss together. Arrange in a single layer and roast in the hot oven for 15 minutes, turning once halfway through.

Cool slightly, but not so much that the honey and sugar set firm on the foil.

Tip into a blender and add 100ml of cold water. Blend until smooth, then gradually add more water until you reach a soupy, but not too loose, consistency.

Add the lime juice and a pinch of salt, mix and then taste to see if you need more of either.

Before serving, chill in the fridge for at least 2 hours. Taste again before serving, as chilling will knock back the flavours.

Serve garnished with mint leaves.

\\\ TIP ///

Serve the soup with ice cream, yoghurt or soured cream. Instead of adding water and making it into soup, try the puréed peach in a Bellini cocktail – just add a spoonful to a glass of fizz.

CRUNCHY TOPS & SWIRLY SWIRLS

GARLIC YOGHURT

SERVES 4–6 as a topping
PREP TIME: 5 MINS
WF · GF · V

250g thick **Greek yoghurt**

1 clove of **garlic**, blanched in boiling water for 3 minutes, then crushed to a paste

salt

An incredibly simple way with yoghurt which works deliciously with Indian and Middle Eastern soups.

Thoroughly mix together the yoghurt, garlic and a pinch of salt. Taste and decide if you'd like more salt. If the sauce is too thick for your purposes, thin it with a little cold water, adding it a tablespoon at a time.

\\\\ TIP ////

For a richer flavour, add a spoonful of extra virgin olive oil to the yoghurt. For more sourness, add a squeeze of fresh lemon juice. Depending on what you're serving it with, add a little finely chopped dill, mint or parsley, some paprika or black pepper.

CRUNCHY TOPS & SWIRLY SWIRLS

RAITA

SERVES 4–6 as a topping or dip
PREP TIME: 5 MINS • COOK TIME: 2 MINS
WF · GF · V

150g **cucumber**, about 8cm of a cucumber

200g **thick Greek-style plain yoghurt**

2 tablespoons **roughly chopped fresh coriander leaves**

leaves from 1 sprig of **fresh mint**, finely chopped

1 teaspoon **cumin seeds**

salt and **freshly ground black pepper**

> \\\ **TIP** ///
> Try any combination of sliced onion, green chilli, diced tomato, grated carrot or ginger on top.

Raita is a cooling yoghurt sauce or dip, and is wonderful with Indian-style spicy or lentil-based soups, like dal (see pages 70 and 98), or as a sauce for barbecued chicken or grilled red meat.

There are dozens of different styles – try this recipe, or use it as a base for exploring other flavours. If you add a couple of cloves of garlic, crushed to a paste with a little salt, plus some fresh dill, and omit the cumin and coriander, you've made Greek tzatziki or Turkish caçik, instead.

Halve the cucumber and scrape out the seeds, then finely dice or coarsely grate it. Place in a bowl with the yoghurt, coriander leaves, mint and a pinch of salt and pepper. Stir, then taste to see if it needs more salt.

Toast the cumin seeds in a dry pan for a minute or so, until fragrant. Remove from the heat and grind roughly. Sprinkle over the raita, along with a little more black pepper, and serve.

TAHINI WITH MINT

SERVES 4 as a topping
PREP TIME: 5 MINS
WF · GF · DF · V · Ve

. . . .

Tahini is a paste made from roasted sesame seeds and one of the main ingredients in hummus. Use this on top of Middle Eastern soups, on the roasted red pepper soup on page 34, or as a nutty, garlicky salad dressing. Dedicated to John's friend Ovid, King of Hummus.

. . . .

2 tablespoons **tahini**

1 small clove of **garlic**, crushed to a paste (blanch in boiling water for 3 minutes before crushing for a more mellow flavour)

2 tablespoons **finely chopped mint leaves**

1 teaspoon **lemon juice**

a pinch of **salt**

2–3 tablespoons **cold water**

Stir together all the ingredients apart from the water, then gradually add the water to thin the sauce. Use a whisk if necessary, as tahini can be very thick and the sauce should be smooth. Taste and add more salt, mint or lemon juice, if you like.

HARISSA

MAKES 1 small jar

PREP TIME: 30 MINS • SOAK TIME: 20 MINS • COOK TIME: 15 MINS

WF • GF • DF • V • Ve

. . . .

Once you've started making this North African chilli paste, you will always want to have a jar in the fridge – swirl it through soups, into yoghurt, add it to cheese dishes, dollop it on eggs...

. . . .

4 finger-length **fresh red chillies**

1 teaspoon **caraway seeds**

1 teaspoon **coriander seeds**

1 teaspoon **cumin seeds**

2 cloves of **garlic**, crushed (blanch in boiling water for 3 minutes before crushing for a more mellow flavour)

1 large **medium-hot dried chilli** (**ancho** or **chipotle** work well), split and soaked in freshly boiled water for 20 minutes

½ teaspoon **sherry vinegar**

zest of ½ an **unwaxed lemon**

4 tablespoons **extra virgin olive oil**

salt

Hold the fresh red chillies directly over a gas ring and cook, turning, until blistered and blackened all over. Alternatively, preheat the grill to its highest setting, halve the chillies and grill, skin side up, until blackened. Seal the blackened chillies in a sandwich bag and leave to steam and cool.

Toast the caraway, coriander and cumin seeds in a dry pan over a medium heat, until fragrant. Remove from the heat and tip into a pestle and mortar. Grind to a fine powder, then add the crushed garlic.

Wearing gloves, peel the blackened skin from the cooked fresh chillies, remove and discard the seeds and stems and place the flesh in the mortar. Remove the seeds, ribs and stem from the rehydrated chilli, chop into small pieces, then add to the mortar. Grind everything to a paste, then add the vinegar, lemon zest, oil and a pinch of salt, and mix.

Use immediately, or store in the fridge in a sealed sterilized jar, with a thin layer of oil on top, for up to 2 weeks.

. . . . **173**

AÏOLI

SERVES 4–6 as a topping
PREP TIME: 15 MINS
WF · GF · DF · V

2 very fresh **egg yolks**, at room
   temperature
a pinch of **English mustard powder**
1–2 cloves of **garlic**, crushed to a paste
   (blanch in boiling water for 3 minutes
   before crushing for a more mellow
   flavour)
125ml **olive oil**
125ml **flavourless oil (sunflower,
   vegetable** or **groundnut)**
1 tablespoon freshly squeezed
   lemon juice
fine salt

This sauce should be pungent and rich with garlic, but too much and it becomes overwhelming. Choose a very light olive oil, as anything bitter will make the sauce taste bitter too. Try this dolloped into Mediterranean fish or vegetable soups.

Place the egg yolks in a bowl with the mustard powder and a pinch of salt. Add the garlic gradually to taste while whisking together until smooth and combined.

Mix together the two oils, then add 1 teaspoon of the oil mixture to the egg yolks. Mix thoroughly with the whisk, then continue adding a teaspoon of oil at a time, until an emulsion forms – this means the egg yolks and oil will combine smoothly, becoming thicker and creamier. After about half the oil is incorporated into the aïoli, you can start adding it in larger quantities, a couple of tablespoons at a time.

Once all the oil is incorporated, you should have a smooth yellow sauce the texture of mayonnaise. Add 1 teaspoon of the lemon juice and whisk that in, then taste and decide if you would like to add more salt, lemon or even crushed blanched garlic.

\\\ TIP ///
Add chopped fresh herbs that suit
the soup you're serving it with:
tarragon or parsley for chicken, or
basil for Mediterranean dishes.

SWEET CHILLI SAUCE

MAKES 1 jar
PREP TIME: 5 MINS • COOK TIME: 8 MINS
WF • GF • DF • V • Ve

The classic Thai dipping sauce is very quick and easy to make at home. Leave out the seeds if you prefer a milder sauce. Serve this with the tom yum (yum yum) on page 22 or the tom kha gai on page 81, or splash a little on to congee (see page 102).

2 tablespoons **cornflour**

4 tablespoons **water**

2 cloves of **garlic**

2 **medium hot red chillies**

125g **sugar**

50ml **white wine vinegar**

1 teaspoon **fine salt**

Whisk the cornflour together with 2 tablespoons of the water, until smooth, then set aside. Place the rest of the ingredients and the remaining water in a blender and blitz until smooth.

Pour into a small non-reactive pan and set over a medium heat. Bring to a simmer and let bubble for 3 or 4 minutes (don't let it boil over), then add the cornflour mixture and cook for another 3 minutes, to thicken slightly. Remove from the heat.

This is ready to use as soon as it has cooled, or, if storing, pour into a clean sterilized 250ml jar or bottle while still hot, and seal. This will keep sealed in the fridge for over a month.

\ \ \ **TIP** / / /

Add 4 or 5 lightly bruised whole cloves of garlic to the hot pan for garlicky chilli oil.

CHILLI OIL

MAKES 1 litre
PREP TIME: 10 MINS • COOK TIME: 2 MINS
MATURING TIME: 2 WEEKS
WF · GF · DF · V · Ve

. . . .

This adds a savoury, earthy, warming layer to almost any vegetable or meat soup. Keep some spare, to drizzle on your pizza.

. . . .

1 litre **extra virgin olive oil**

10 whole **black peppercorns**

zest of 1 **lemon**, shaved using a peeler

5 **bay leaves**, ideally fresh

8–10 **long red chillies**, a mixture of sizes
    (smaller chillies tend to be hotter)

1 tablespoon freshly squeezed **lemon juice**

a generous pinch of **flaky sea salt**

Sterilise a 1-litre heatproof glass jar or wide-mouthed bottle with a lid.

Place a little of the oil in a large pan and set over a medium heat. Add the peppercorns, lemon zest and bay leaves, then lightly bruise the chillies, but leave them whole, and add them to the pan too. Cook for just a minute or two, then add the rest of the oil, with the lemon juice and salt. Mix, then allow the oil to warm until hot but nowhere near boiling.

Remove from the heat. While still hot, carefully pour into the prepared jar or bottle and seal. Leave for a couple of weeks, somewhere cool and away from bright light, shaking every few days. The longer you leave it the better the flavours will develop. It will keep for several months.

. . . . **177**

GUACAMOLE

SERVES 4 as a topping or dip
PREP TIME: 5 MINS
WF · GF · DF · V · Ve

· ·

1 ripe **avocado**, peeled and pitted

juice of ½ a **lime**

5 **cherry tomatoes**, seeded and
    finely chopped

1 tablespoon finely chopped seeded
    fresh red chilli, or to taste

1 small **shallot**, very finely diced

2 tablespoons **chopped coriander leaves**

a pinch of **salt**

Although often thought of as a dip, guacamole makes a great topping, adding a creamy, spicy kick to South American-style soups, like the Brexican on page 53 or the posole on page 58.

· ·

Combine all the ingredients in a bowl and mix together, mashing the avocado as you go. Taste and add more lime, chilli or salt, if necessary. If not serving straight away, press a layer of cling film on to the surface of the guacamole to stop it from turning brown.

GREMOLATA

SERVES 4 as a topping
PREP TIME: 5 MINS
WF · GF · DF · V · Ve

a generous handful of **fresh flat-leaf parsley leaves**

zest of an **unwaxed lemon**

1 clove of **garlic**, blanched in boiling water for 3 minutes

TIP
Try gremolata made with coriander and lime, or tarragon and lemon.

Gremolata is a parsley, lemon zest and garlic garnish, traditionally used on top of osso bucco, an Italian braised veal dish. It is perfect for topping meaty soups like the lamb and barley pearly king (of soups) on page 85 or the sausage soups on pages 57 and 74, or to add freshness to sweet vegetable soups like the roasted red pepper on page 34 or the roasted squash on page 89.

Wash and thoroughly dry the parsley – if wet, the parsley can make the gremolata stick together in clumps. Chop the leaves as finely as possible – do it as much as you think you can and then chop a bit more.

Add the lemon zest, then use a fine grater to grate in the blanched garlic. Mix well.

Gremolata should be used the day it is made.

SALSA VERDE

SERVES 4 as a topping or sauce
PREP TIME: 10 MINS
WF · GF · DF

1 small bunch of **fresh parsley**, leaves only

1 small bunch of **fresh basil**, leaves only

4 **anchovy fillets** in oil, drained

1 clove of **garlic**, crushed to a paste
(blanch in boiling water for 3 minutes
before crushing for a more mellow
flavour)

1 heaped tablespoon **capers in brine**,
drained, rinsed and finely chopped

¼ teaspoon **Dijon mustard**

1 **shallot**, very finely diced

1 teaspoon **sherry vinegar** or
red wine vinegar

5 tablespoons **extra virgin olive oil**

Salsa verde played an important part in our early days – it was on our menu from the first day at Carnaby Street and, in his column, John offered every Metro reader a free jar if they tweeted him. Many did, and it took seven of us three days to make enough jars.

This is a pretty traditional recipe, a powerful parsley, garlic, caper and anchovy sauce often served with grilled meat but fabulous with Tuscan sausage soup (see page 74) or with pancotto (see page 82). Once mastered, try it with wild garlic, chives or tarragon. Making this by hand in a pestle and mortar gives a pleasing chunky texture, but you can, of course, just throw everything into the food processor.

Place the herbs and anchovies in a pestle and mortar and pummel to a pulp. Add the garlic and pummel a bit more, then stir in the capers, mustard, shallot, vinegar and olive oil.

Serve straight away, or keep in the fridge for a few days, stored in a sealed sterilized container, with a thin layer of oil on top.

ZHOUG

SERVES 4 as a topping
PREP TIME: 5 MINS
WF · GF · DF · V · Ve

3 tablespoons **roughly chopped fresh coriander leaves**

1 tablespoon **roughly chopped fresh parsley leaves**

2 cloves of **garlic**, blanched in boiling water for 3 minutes

¾ teaspoon **ground cumin**

3 tablespoons **extra virgin olive oil**

2 medium **fresh green chillies**, seeded

a generous pinch of **sugar**

3 **cardamom pods**, shells discarded, seeds ground

a very small pinch of **ground cloves**

½ teaspoon **lemon juice**

1 teaspoon **water**

a pinch of **chilli powder** (optional)

salt and **freshly ground black pepper**

Zhoug is a green chilli sauce from Yemen, delicious with Middle Eastern and lentil- or chickpea-based soups and curries. It's also very good with eggs or stirred into thick Greek yoghurt.

Blitz everything except the water, salt, black pepper and chilli powder to a rough purée. It needs to be of pouring consistency, so add a little water if necessary. Taste, and add plenty of salt and black pepper. It should be hot, garlicky and fragrant. Add the chilli powder if your green chillies aren't very hot (a common problem with supermarket chillies).

Serve straight away, or keep in the fridge for a few days, stored in a sealed sterilized container, with a thin layer of oil on top.

WHIPPED FETA

SERVES 4–6 as a topping
PREP TIME: 5 MINS
WF · GF · V

. . . .

100g **feta**, crumbled into small pieces
100g **Greek** or **Greek-style yoghurt**

Use this light and creamy topping on tomato, sweet pepper or lentil-based soups.

. . . .

Place the ingredients into a food processor or blender and blend together until completely smooth.

Use immediately, or keep, covered, in the fridge for 48 hours.

\ \ \ \ TIP / / / /

Use whipped feta in soups, or as a crostini topping, with oregano and tomatoes, or tangy sumac.

LABNEH

SERVES 4 as a topping or dip
PREP TIME: 5 MINS • DRAINING TIME: OVERNIGHT
WF • GF • V

....

200g **full-fat Greek** or
   Greek-style yoghurt
salt

Labneh is a creamy Middle Eastern cheese made from strained yoghurt. It's incredibly quick and easy to make, and very versatile – as well as dolloped into soups, it can be spread on bread or used as a dip. Use in place of yoghurt or feta on top of soup.

....

\\\ TIP ///

Serve labneh topped with a drizzle of good olive oil, fresh thyme leaves, za'atar spice blend, dukkah (see page 190), chilli flakes or a little hot harissa (see page 173).

Line a sieve with clean muslin or cheesecloth (or, at a push, kitchen paper). Set the sieve over a bowl. Mix a pinch of salt into the yoghurt, then pour into the lined sieve.

Leave to drain in the fridge for 8 hours or overnight. When ready, it will be very thick, having lost lots of liquid. Exactly how much labneh you end up with depends on how thick the yoghurt was to begin with – it may lose up to a quarter of its weight in liquid.

Labneh will keep in the fridge for 3 or 4 days.

PESTO

SERVES 4–6 as a topping or with pasta

PREP TIME: 5 MINS

WF · GF

50g **pine nuts**

50g **basil leaves**

1 clove of **garlic**, blanched in boiling water for 3 minutes

30g freshly grated **Parmesan**

150ml **extra virgin olive oil**

¼ teaspoon **lemon juice** (optional)

salt

\\\ TIP ///

Try different styles of pesto: coriander and pistachio, or dill, parsley and almond; use cashews instead of pine nuts; add chives, lemon zest and walnuts.

John's wife Katie first tasted pesto while inter-railing in Italy. 'What is this grass they have put on my spaghetti?' she asked herself. Now pesto is the vanilla ice cream of pasta dressings. But it is just as good with soup.

A dollop of freshly made pesto brightens up many soups, but is particularly good with the green crunch of spring minestrone (see page 112) or with any of the Italian soups we've included here, especially those with meatballs.

Gently toast the pine nuts in a dry pan for a couple of minutes. Use a pestle and mortar to grind the basil leaves until pulpy, then add the garlic, pine nuts and Parmesan and grind to a paste. Next add the oil and a little pinch of salt. Mix together and taste. A little lemon juice can brighten the flavour, so decide if you'd like to add it now.

Pesto will keep for a week or so in the fridge if kept in a sterilized sealed container and covered with a layer of extra virgin olive oil. Whenever using pesto, add it once the rest of the dish is cooked and off the heat, as cooking it will spoil its flavour.

ROASTY TOASTY NUTS

SERVES 4 as a topping

PREP TIME: 2 MINS • COOK TIME: 7 MINS

WF • GF • DF • V • Ve

. . . .

100g **mixed un-roasted, unsalted nuts**, chopped into pieces if necessary

Add flavour, texture and goodness to even the simplest soup. You can roast nuts in the oven or on the stovetop – Rebecca prefers the stovetop, as she can keep a close eye on whether they are burning or not.

. . . .

If using the oven, heat it to 180°C/350°F/gas mark 4; spread the nuts out on a baking tray and cook for 5–7 minutes, depending on the size of the nuts, until golden. On the stovetop, set a dry pan over a low heat. When hot, add the nuts and cook, tossing frequently, for 2–4 minutes, until brown and toasted.

If you want to coat the nuts with spices you can use either water, water and beaten egg white, or water and melted butter to get the spices to stick to the nuts. Just mix a couple of tablespoons of each together with your spices (paprika, sugar, salt, cumin, za'atar, chilli, etc) and toss the nuts thoroughly in the mixture before roasting in the oven.

ROMESCO SAUCE

SERVES 4 as a topping or dip, with leftovers
PREP TIME: 5 MINS • COOK TIME: 8 MINS
DF • V • Ve

2 **red peppers**

5 tablespoons **extra virgin olive oil**, plus
   a splash for frying

50g **cherry tomatoes**, seeded

2 cloves of **garlic**, crushed

1 slice of **day-old white bread**,
   crusts removed

50g **ground almonds**

½ tablespoon **sherry vinegar** or **red
   wine vinegar**

½ teaspoon **sweet smoked paprika**

salt

This tangy, smoky pepper sauce is wonderful with soups like the cauliflower and chickpeas (see page 94) or the roasted red pepper (see page 34); it's also very good with roasted onions or grilled fish.

Hold the whole red peppers directly over a gas ring and cook, turning, until blistered and blackened all over. Alternatively, preheat the grill to its highest setting, halve the peppers and grill, skin side up, until blackened in the same way.

When done, seal the peppers in a sandwich bag and leave to steam and cool.

Meanwhile put a splash of oil into a small pan over a medium heat and tip in the tomatoes and garlic. Cook for 2 minutes, then remove from the heat.

Tear the bread into small pieces and place in a hot, dry pan over a medium heat. Cook for 3 or 4 minutes, until beginning to dry out, then add the ground almonds and cook for a couple of minutes longer, stirring all the time so they don't catch. Remove from the heat.

Add the tomatoes and garlic to the bread mixture. Add the remaining oil, the vinegar, paprika and a pinch of salt.

The peppers should now be cool enough to handle. Rub off the blackened skins and discard, then remove the stalks, seeds and ribs. (Don't rinse them, as you'll lose the flavour.) Chop into bite-sized pieces and add to the breadcrumb mixture. Blend until fairly smooth, then taste. Romesco should be sweet, sour, salty and rich; add a little more salt and vinegar if necessary.

This will keep in a sterilized jar, covered with a thin layer of oil, in the fridge for up to a week.

> ### \\\\\ TIP /////
>
> Try adding a handful of skinned hazelnuts to the pan with the ground almonds. You can make a spicy version of this sauce by adding a couple of rehydrated dried chillies or a pinch of chilli powder.

DUKKAH

SERVES 4–6 as a topping, with leftovers
PREP TIME: 5 MINS · COOK TIME: 10 MINS
WF · GF · DF · V · Ve

50g **unsalted pistachios**
75g **blanched hazelnuts**
25g **blanched almonds**
1 teaspoon **fennel seeds**
1 teaspoon **cumin seeds**
10 whole **black peppercorns**
2 teaspoons **coriander seeds**
2 tablespoons **sesame seeds**
½ teaspoon **sweet paprika**
½ teaspoon **sumac**
a tiny pinch of **fine salt**

Dukkah is an Egyptian spice-and-nut blend, and is used as a both a seasoning and a topping. Not only is it wonderful on top of soups like black dal (see page 70), roasted squash (see page 89), or red lentils with spinach, yoghurt, pomegranate & crispy onions (see page 77), but you can also use it to add complexity to salads, roasted vegetables, poached eggs and on top of dips, or as a crust for baked fish.

Heat the oven to 220°C/425°F/gas mark 7. Place the nuts on a baking tray in a single layer and pop them into the oven for 5 or 6 minutes, until golden brown.

Toast the whole spices and sesame seeds in a dry pan over a low heat for 3 or 4 minutes, until fragrant.

Allow both to cool, then place in the bowl of a food processor along with the sweet paprika, sumac and a tiny pinch of salt. Blitz to your preferred texture – dukkah can be very fine and sandy or quite textured. Taste the dukkah and add more salt if necessary. This will keep for a couple of weeks in a sealed container.

PUFFED &
POPPED SEEDS

SERVES 4 as a topping or dip
PREP TIME: 5 MINS
WF · GF · DF · V · Ve

· ·

40g **pumpkin seeds**
1–2 tablespoons mixed **sesame seeds**
   and **linseeds**

Roasted pumpkin seeds are also known as pepitas. As well as being an addictive-yet-wholesome crunchy top for soups, especially South American soups like the Brexican on page 53, the chilled avocado on page 121, or the super soup on page 25, they are scrumptious in salads or as a pre-dinner snack.

· ·

\\\\ **TIP** ////

Depending on what soup you're using them in, spice up your seeds by tossing, while still hot, with some of the following: a pinch of flaky sea salt plus a pinch of ground cumin, chilli powder, smoked paprika, ground coriander or cayenne pepper.

Place a frying pan over a medium heat. Tip in the seeds and allow to cook for 2–3 minutes, until they begin to pop and puff up. Allow the pumpkin seeds to brown just slightly, giving them a nutty flavour, then remove from the heat, making sure they don't burn. Add any spices (see tip) while the seeds are still piping hot.

·   **CRUNCHY TOPS & SWIRLY SWIRLS**   ·   **191**

FRAZZLED CHORIZO, BACON OR PANCETTA

SERVES 4 as a topping
PREP TIME: 5 MINS • COOK TIME: 10 MINS
WF • **GF** (but check the chorizo) • **DF**

flavourless oil
200g **pancetta**, **smoked bacon** or
   cooking chorizo, cut into cubes or
   small pieces

It's hard to think of a savoury soup that wouldn't benefit from a handful of hot, crunchy, salty meat scattered on top.

Set a wide frying pan over a high heat and add a splash of oil – the meat will release its own fat, so you don't need much. When hot, add the meat. Cook, stirring often, for up to 10 minutes, until really crisp. At this point, keep a close eye, as there's a thin line between deliciously crunchy and burnt to a cinder.

Remove from the heat, then use a slotted spoon to lift out the meat and leave the fat behind.

Serve scattered on to soup straight away, while hot.

CRISPY ONIONS

SERVES 4 as a topping
PREP TIME: 5 MINS · COOK TIME: 30–35 MINS
WF · GF · DF · V · Ve

3 tablespoons **flavourless oil**
2 onions, finely sliced into half moons
salt

You can't rush this one. If too hot, the onions will burn, but cooked long and slow they will caramelize and crisp right up. Use on top of lentil, squash or root vegetable soups.

Pour the oil into a wide frying pan set over the lowest heat possible. Add the onions and cook really slowly, stirring often, until deep brown, nutty, sweet and really crisp, up to 35 minutes.

Lift out and drain off any excess oil on kitchen paper. Toss with a little pinch of salt before using.

PICKLED GINGER

MAKES 1 jar

PREP TIME: 5 MINS • SALTING TIME: 30 MINUTES • COOK TIME: 5 MINS

WF • GF • DF • V • Ve

100–150g **fresh ginger**, peeled

2½ tablespoons **caster sugar**

100ml **rice or white wine vinegar**

200ml **water**

fine salt

Japanese pickled ginger, gari, is made with either pink shiso leaf or pink food colouring, which gives it its distinctive colour. Unless you can get young and tender ginger from a Japanese supermarket, you will need to salt the ginger for 30 minutes before use, to tame its fiery flavour.

Slice the ginger as thinly as possible, ideally using the finest setting on a mandolin—you want the ginger to be so thin that it is almost transparent. Place it in a bowl and sprinkle with a pinch of salt; leave for 30 minutes.

Place the sugar, vinegar, water and 1 teaspoon of salt in a small non-reactive pan and bring to the boil, stirring to dissolve the salt and sugar. Tip the ginger into the pan, and cook for a couple of minutes.

Remove from the heat, lift out the ginger with a slotted spoon and place it in a clean, sterilized jar. Top the jar up with the pickling brine. The pickle will be ready to use in 15 minutes, but will keep in the fridge for a month or more.

TIP

Serve this with the miso and tofu on page 42 or with the soba noodles on page 126.

CROUTONS

SERVES 4 as a topping
PREP TIME: 5 MINS · COOK TIME: 15 MINS
DF · V · Ve (if made with oil)

400g **slightly stale bread**
75g melted **butter** or **olive oil**

Different bread makes different kinds of croutons: sourdough croutons are particularly crunchy and full of flavour, while a farmhouse loaf makes croutons that will melt into your soup (wholemeal croutons are a wee bit worthy for us though…). It's up to you what shape you go for – traditional French soups suit thin, angular slices of baguette, while classic tomato soup looks great topped with rugged, roughly cut, square croutons.

 **TIP**

Use olive oil if you're topping a fresh-flavoured Mediterranean soup, but butter is best for creamy dishes. Rub the bread slices with raw garlic before baking for subtly garlicky croutons.

Heat the oven to 180°C/350°F/gas mark 4.

Cut the bread into slices and trim off the crusts, or, if using a baguette, cut thin slices on an angle. Brush each slice with melted butter or oil, on both sides. Lay the baguette slices on a baking tray, or chop the bread into neat squares or rough chunks and then spread them in a single layer on a baking tray.

Place in the oven for 10–15 minutes, turning once, or until crisp and golden. Remove and keep warm. Serve on top of the soup.

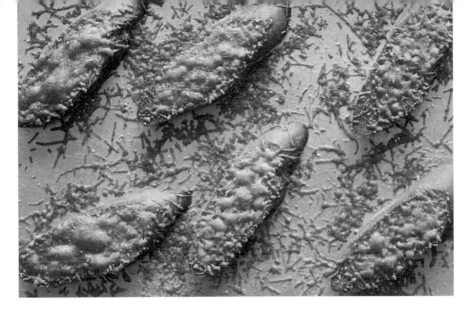

PARMESAN CRUNCH TOASTS

SERVES 4–6 as a side
PREP TIME: 5 MINS · COOK TIME: 10 MINS

½ a **long sourdough baguette**

1 clove of **garlic**, halved, for rubbing (optional)

melted **butter** or **olive oil**, for brushing

about 1 heaped teaspoon freshly grated **Parmesan** per slice of baguette

Posh, crunchy cheese on toast, basically.

Heat the oven to 200°C/400°F/gas mark 6. Cut the baguette into 1-cm slices, cutting on an angle. Rub each slice with the cut side of the garlic, if using. Brush lightly with melted butter or olive oil. Place on a baking tray, then top each slice with grated Parmesan. Slide into the oven and cook for 10 minutes, or until the bread is crisp and golden brown. Serve while warm.

PANGRATTATO

SERVES 4 as a topping
PREP TIME: 5 MINS • COOK TIME: 8 MINS
DF • V • Ve

Pangrattato is halfway between breadcrumbs and croutons, given a little Italian love with the addition of olive oil, garlic and herbs. It is brilliant at adding texture to a soup when used as a topping (it also makes a great lazy supper when added to cooked spaghetti with a splash more olive oil).

150g **slightly stale bread**, crusts removed, processed to breadcrumbs

1 clove of **garlic**, crushed

zest from ½ an **unwaxed lemon**

2 tablespoons **olive oil**

2 tablespoons **very finely chopped fresh parsley**

flaky sea salt and **freshly ground black pepper**

Heat the oven to 200°C/400°F/gas mark 6. Toss the breadcrumbs, crushed garlic, lemon zest and a pinch of pepper together, making sure the garlic doesn't clump in one place. Add the oil and toss again.

Spread the crumbs out in a single layer on a baking tray and slide into the oven. Cook for 5–8 minutes, until the crumbs are golden brown and fragrant, turning once halfway through.

Remove from the oven, cool slightly, taste and decide if you want to add a pinch of salt, then stir in the chopped parsley. Use straight away, or keep in a sealed box for a day or two; crisp up again in the oven before use. (If making in advance and storing, don't add the parsley until serving.)

CRUNCHY CHEESE CRUMBS

SERVES 4 as a topping
PREP TIME: 5 MINS • COOK TIME: 10 MINS
WF • GF • V

These crumbly little nuggets of cheese are worryingly addictive. Try them on top of the wintery tomato soup on page 78 or any vegetable soup, like courgette and green herb (see page 38) or celeriac and crispy sage (see page 69).

100g **halloumi**

flavourless oil, for greasing

Heat the oven to 200°C/400°F/gas mark 6. Chop the halloumi into 5-mm pieces – they don't need to be even, but they do need to be small.

Using kitchen paper dipped in a little flavourless cooking oil, very lightly grease a nonstick baking tray or, even better, a silicone baking mat. Spread the pieces of cheese out in a single layer and cook for 10 minutes in the hot oven – they are ready when they are almost all golden brown and crisp. Remove from the oven and use a spatula to slide or scrape them off the tray. Use straight away, while hot.

\\\ TIP ///

Pangrattato is very adaptable – when making the breadcrumbs, add finely chopped anchovies or fresh chilli; add chopped nuts like almonds, walnuts or pine nuts; or switch the herbs – try finely chopped rosemary, thyme or basil. You could even add it to the crunchy cheese crumbs too.

SIDES

SPEEDY SODA BREAD

MAKES 1 loaf

PREP TIME: 15 MINS • COOK TIME: 40 MINS

V

100g **wholemeal flour**

350g **plain flour**, plus extra for dusting

1 teaspoon **fine salt**

1 teaspoon **bicarbonate of soda**

300ml **buttermilk** or **live yoghurt**

4 tablespoons **milk**, if necessary

a handful of **oats** (optional)

This is super-quick to make, as it requires no rising time, a fail-safe for those days when you realize too late that the bread bin is empty.

Heat the oven to 220°C/425°F/gas mark 7.

Mix the flours, salt and bicarbonate of soda together in a large bowl. Make a well in the middle, then pour in the buttermilk and stir into the dry ingredients. The aim is for a soft, almost-but-not-quite sticky dough. Depending on how thin your buttermilk is, you may need some or all of the milk as well.

Shape the soft dough into a fairly neat ball. Dust a baking tray with flour and place the dough on it. Pat it out slightly, to form a round loaf about 25cm across. Dust with oats, if using, and a little more flour, then use a serrated knife to cut a shallow cross in the top of the loaf.

Pop the loaf into the oven straight away and bake for 40 minutes. When ready, the crust will be a nutty golden brown and the loaf will sound hollow when tapped on the base. Remove from the oven and let it cool before tearing into it – this loaf is wonderful warm with butter, but if you cut it while hot, its moisture will escape as steam.

TIP

For a darker, caramel note to the bread, whisk a tablespoon of black treacle into the buttermilk before adding it to the flour.

CRUSTY WHITE ROLLS

MAKES 6–8 rolls

PREP TIME: 20 MINS • RISE TIME: 1½ HOURS • COOK TIME: 20 MINS

DF (if made with olive oil) • V • Ve (if made with sugar)

1 tablespoon **dried active yeast**

300ml **tepid water**

1 teaspoon **honey** or **sugar** (any kind)

1 tablespoon **olive oil** or **melted butter**

1 ½ teaspoons **fine salt**

500g **strong white flour** (or **wholemeal bread flour** to make crusty wholemeal rolls), plus more for dusting

Bake, break, butter, dunk.

Whisk together the yeast, tepid water and honey or sugar. Leave to stand for 10 minutes to wake up the yeast; the liquid will develop a frothy head. Whisk in the oil or butter.

In a large bowl, mix together the yeast mixture, salt and flour, first using a spoon, then your hands, until you get a rough, craggy dough. Flour a clean work surface and knead the dough for around 8 minutes (or use a mixer with a dough hook, but only knead for 5 minutes).

Place the dough in a clean, oiled bowl and cover with a clean damp tea towel. Leave somewhere warm to rise, for about an hour; it needs to double in size.

When the dough has risen, line a large baking tray, or two baking trays, with baking paper and dust with flour. Knock back the dough (punch back to its original size), then divide into 6 large rolls, or 8 smaller rolls. Shape into rounds, tucking the dough in on itself, and place on the prepared baking tray(s) neat side up.

Drape the damp tea towel back over the baking tray(s) and leave to rise again for 30 minutes. Heat the oven to 240°C/475°F/gas mark 9 and place a roasting tin in the bottom to heat up. Boil the kettle.

When ready to bake, carefully pour about 2cm of boiling water into the very hot roasting tin, filling the oven with steam. Swiftly uncover the rolls and put them into the hot oven on the baking tray.

Bake for 15–20 minutes, or until the rolls have a golden crust and sound hollow when tapped on the base. Cool on a rack to avoid a soggy bottom developing. These can be served warm or cold.

RYE BREAD

MAKES 1 loaf

PREP TIME: 20 MINS • RISE TIME: 4–6 HOURS • COOK TIME: 35 MINS

DF • V • Ve

400ml **tepid water**

1 tablespoon **dried active yeast**

2 tablespoons **molasses** or **black treacle**

400g **rye flour**

100g **strong wholemeal bread flour**

1 teaspoon **fine salt**

plain flour, for dusting and kneading

John: As I am writing this, Saskia, our PunBandit, is round for dinner. Saskia says follow the recipe and things won't go awry. She wanted me to create a soup that goes with it called Rye Me a River but I said that would be stoupid.

Dark, dense and savoury rye bread is especially excellent with fish soups like lohikietto (see page 154) and smoked haddock chowder (see page 15). It makes very good toast and is wonderful with either butter or cream cheese, or both. It needs a long rise, but can be completely ignored during, so the time you're actually involved in making it is very short.

Pour the water into a jug and whisk in the yeast and molasses or treacle. Leave to stand for 10 minutes to activate the yeast; the mixture will develop a frothy head.

Stir together the rye and bread flours in a large mixing bowl. Add the salt and then the yeast mixture. Mix, using a spoon at first and then your hands, until a rough, craggy dough forms.

Generously flour a clean work surface with plain flour, and flour your hands too. Tip the dough out and knead for a couple of minutes. (It doesn't need much kneading, as this bread doesn't contain as much gluten as wheat-only breads.) Once the dough is smooth – it will still be a bit sticky – shape it into a neat ball, tucking the dough under itself so that it is very tidy on top. Dust a proving basket, if you have one, with flour and turn the bread dough into it, neatest side down. If you don't have a basket, line a baking tray with baking paper and place the dough on it, neat side up (this will result in a wider, flatter loaf, but this doesn't matter).

Cover the proving basket with a clean, slightly damp tea towel, or cover the baking tray with a large up-turned bowl, leaving enough room for the dough to rise without touching and sticking to it. Leave to prove at room temperature for 4–6 hours, depending on the how warm or cool the room is.

\\\\ TIP ////

Add 50g of mixed seeds to the dough – sunflower and pumpkin seeds are good for texture – or try 1 tablespoon of caraway or fennel seeds, or chopped nuts. For added tang, swap 100ml of the water for 100ml of buttermilk.

Like wheat breads, the dough needs to more or less double in size, but will probably take much longer to do so.

When ready to cook, heat the oven to 240°C/475°F/gas mark 9. Boil the kettle and place a roasting tin in the bottom of the oven.

Uncover the risen dough and, if using a basket, turn out on to a baking tray lined with baking paper. Use a serrated knife to slash the top, either with a cross or a square, and dust with a little more plain flour.

Before placing the bread dough in the oven, carefully pour about 2cm of boiling water into the very hot roasting tin, to fill the oven with steam. Working quickly, put the loaf into the oven and cook for 30–35 minutes, by which time the bread should be deep brown on top and sound hollow when the base is tapped. Unlike most wheat breads, it won't rise much in the oven.

Leave to cool completely on a rack before cutting into it, otherwise the bread's moisture will escape as hot steam, and the loaf will go stale faster.

POSH FOUR-CHEESE TOASTIES

SERVES 1

PREP TIME: 5 MINS • COOK TIME: 5 MINS

V

butter, for spreading

2 slices of **good-quality bread**, something sturdy like **sourdough**

40g of mixed **grated mature red Leicester** and **strong mature Cheddar**

1 tablespoon **grated Gruyère**

20g **mozzarella**, shredded

Using good-quality bread and really tasty cheese is the trick here – you can use cheap or farmhouse-style white bread, but the sandwich will have more of a student-y vibe. This recipe can be turned into either a grilled cheese sandwich, or open-faced cheese-on-toast.

If making a toasted cheese sandwich: butter one side of each of the two slices of bread. Mix the cheeses together and arrange on top of one of the slices of bread, with the butter facing down. Sandwich with the other slice of bread, butter on the outside.

Place a frying pan over a medium heat. Slide the sandwich into the pan and weigh it down with another pan, using the base of the second pan to press the sandwich so that all the bread on the bottom comes into contact with the pan. After 2 or 3 minutes, when the bottom is golden all over, flip the sandwich and repeat.

If making cheese on toast: omit the butter. Heat the grill to medium. Lightly toast the bread slices first, then load them with the cheese mixture. Place under the grill and cook until the cheese is melted and bubbling.

Serve straightaway and, if not serving with soup, with some dill pickles or sweet pickle on the side.

TIP

Match extra fillings with the soup you're serving these with – options include chopped spring onions, diced shallots, chopped kimchi, a smear of hot sauce, cooked chorizo or bacon, pickled chillies, chopped capers or cayenne pepper.

FLATBREADS

MAKES 8

PREP TIME: 25 MINS · RISE TIME: 1 HOUR · COOK TIME: 15 MINS

V · (DF · Ve if garlic butter is omitted)

350ml **tepid water**

1 tablespoon **dried active yeast**

1 tablespoon **sugar**

2 tablespoons **olive oil**, plus extra for
cooking

500g **strong white bread flour**

2 teaspoons **salt**

FOR FLAVOURED FLATBREADS:

mixed seeds: 2 tablespoons **mixed seeds
(toasted sesame, nigella, black onion,
fennel, caraway, sunflower** or
pumpkin)

garlic butter: 3 tablespoons **melted
butter**, plus 1 clove of **garlic**, crushed
to a paste, and 3 tablespoons **very
finely chopped fresh parsley** (or
thyme, rosemary or **tarragon)**

olive oil and za'atar: 3 tablespoons
olive oil mixed with 1 tablespoon
za'atar spice mix

olive oil and paprika: 3 tablespoons
olive oil mixed with 1 teaspoon **hot** or
sweet smoked paprika, plus a pinch
each of **freshly ground black pepper**
and **flaky sea salt**

*Use these easy flatbreads as wraps, for dipping or scooping, or follow one
of the seedy, garlicky or spicy variations below.*

Mix the water, yeast, sugar and olive oil in a jug and leave to stand for 10 minutes.

In a large mixing bowl, add the yeast-water mixture to the flour and salt and mix
thoroughly. (Add the seeds now, if using.) The dough will be fairly sticky at this stage.
On a floured surface, start to knead the dough, using floured hands and knuckles to
stretch the dough out, before folding it back on itself. (If it is really too sticky to do
this, add another tablespoon or two of flour to the mix.) Knead for 10 minutes, by
which time the dough will be smooth and pliable. Place the dough in an oiled bowl,
cover and leave in a warm place for about an hour or until doubled in size.

Once the dough has risen, knock it back, using your hands to squash it back to
roughly its original size. Divide into 8 equally sized balls. Dust a clean work surface
and rolling pin with flour and roll out until 4mm thick and about 20cm in diameter.
Using a fork, gently prick the breads all over, being careful not to poke all the way
through the dough. Set aside for 10 minutes.

Heat a wide frying pan over a medium heat until hot. Have ready a clean tea towel to
wrap the breads in. Pour a splash of olive oil on to a piece of kitchen paper and wipe
around the pan. Place the first bread into the pan and cook for 2 or 3 minutes, until
golden brown bubbles and flecks appear on the bottom. Flip and cook for 2 more
minutes, pressing down gently if the bread puffs up. Remove from the pan when
golden brown bubbles have appeared on that side too, and wrap in the tea towel to
steam and keep warm until the other breads are ready. Wipe the pan with the oiled
kitchen paper again, and cook the rest of the breads in the same way.

If using any of the butter or oil-based toppings, brush over the breads while still
warm, just before serving.

SIDES

\\\ **TIP** ///

For quickie flatbreads, skip
the yeast and all the rising.
Add 2 teaspoons baking
powder to the flour instead.

STOCKS & BROTHS

CHICK-CHICK CHICKEN STOCK

MAKES 750ml–1.5 litres, depending on your pan

PREP TIME: 15 MINS • COOK TIME: 2 HOURS

WF • GF • DF

. . . .

Consider this recipe a basic guide – there are few hard and fast rules when it comes to chicken stock, so if you want to make more, or less, or use other herbs to help the stock suit whatever you have planned for it, feel free – we love to add garlic, rosemary or thyme. The only vegetables to avoid are floury ones like potatoes, turnips and swede which will make the stock cloudy, and anything which might colour the stock, like beetroot.

For a paler, lighter stock, known as white stock, use uncooked chicken bones from the butcher.

. . . .

bones and **leftover meat** from 1 or 2 **whole cooked chickens**, fat and skin removed

2 **onions**, roughly chopped

2 **carrots**, roughly chopped

2 sticks of **celery**, roughly chopped

1 **leek**, roughly chopped

4 or 5 **fresh parsley stalks**

10 **black peppercorns**

a pinch of **salt**

1 **bay leaf**

1–2 litres **boiling water**

Place a very large pan with a lid over a low heat. Add the cooked chicken bones and any meat still attached to them – pulled apart to fit, if necessary – and all the other ingredients. Finish by adding enough freshly boiled water to submerge everything, leaving about 3cm space at the top of the pan. Bring to a gentle simmer, skim off any scum and fat that rises to the surface, then cover and cook for 1½ hours. Uncover for a final 30 minutes of cooking to reduce and concentrate the stock.

Once cooled, store in the fridge for 3 days, or freeze in ice cube trays or ice cube bags.

> **\ \ \ | TIP | / / /**
>
> Don't let the stock boil hard, as this causes the fat to emulsify into the liquid. If gently simmered, once the stock has cooled you will be able to lift the fat from the surface of the stock.

BEEF STOCK

MAKES 1.25–1.5 litres
PREP TIME: 10 MINS • COOK TIME: 3–5 HOURS
WF · GF · DF

This is known as a brown stock, because the bones are roasted before being added to the stock.

Heat the oven to 220°C/425°F/gas mark 7. Place the bones in a roasting tin and cook until browned all over – about 45–55 minutes.

Put the oil into a pan big enough for all the bones, set over a medium heat. Add the onions, carrots and celery and cook until beginning to brown, 15–20 minutes. Don't let them burn, as this will make the stock bitter. Set aside until the bones are ready.

When the bones have browned, add them to the pan, leaving any rendered fat behind in the roasting tin. (Use it for roast potatoes.) Fill the pan with boiling water, covering the bones and vegetables, then add the herbs and peppercorns and bring to a simmer.

Skim off any fat or scum that rises to the surface; do this two or three times throughout the cooking process. Turn the heat down so the stock is barely simmering, then cover and leave for 2–4 hours; the longer the better.

Strain the stock well and discard the bones, herbs and vegetables, again skimming off any fat from the surface (or use a fat separator jug for this). If you want to reduce it, return the strained, skimmed stock to the pan and boil hard.

Store in the fridge for a couple of days, or freeze in ice cube trays or ice cube bags.

2kg **beef** or **high welfare rose veal bones**, raw, cut into manageable pieces by your butcher if possible

1 tablespoon **sunflower** or **vegetable oil**

2 **onions**, chopped into chunks

2 **carrots**, chopped into chunks

2 sticks of **celery**, chopped into chunks

2 **bay leaves**

2 sprigs of **fresh thyme**

6–8 **fresh parsley stalks**

10 **black peppercorns**

\\\\ TIP ////

Freezing stock as ice cubes means you can use as little or as much as you need. Just freeze, then pop out of the tray and into a freezer bag, or use ice cube bags.

FISH STOCK

MAKES about 1 litre
PREP TIME: 15 MINS · COOK TIME: 20–30 MINS
WF · GF · DF

. . . .

Fish stock is one of the quickest stocks to make, taking less than half an hour. It's best to use bones from white or pink fish, like gurnard, trout, bass or bream (you may be able to get them for free from your fishmonger). Avoid using bones from oily fish, as they have a bit too much flavour. Make sure the heads are removed and that they are clean of guts and gills, as they can make stock bitter; rinse off any blood before cooking, for a clearer stock.

Reduce the stock only after removing the fish bones – if the bones cook for too long, the stock will become unpleasantly fishy and bitter.

You can add other flavourings to this basic recipe, depending on what you plan to use it for: sliced fennel, tarragon, fresh oregano, thyme, white wine, a little white wine vinegar, lemon juice and garlic all work. The same recipe works for shellfish stock – just add shells in place of the bones.

500g **clean raw fish bones**

1 litre **water**

1 **onion**, chopped into small pieces

1 **carrot**, chopped into small pieces

2 sticks of **celery**, chopped into small
   pieces

4 whole sprigs of **fresh parsley**

10 **black peppercorns**

a pinch of **salt**

. . . .

Chop or snip the bones into lengths that will fit into your pan. Set the pan over a medium heat and add all the ingredients. Bring to a simmer, then simmer gently for 20 minutes, straining off any scum or fat that rises to the surface. Strain, using the finest strainer you have, and if you want to reduce it, return the liquid to the pan and boil a little longer.

Cool and keep in the fridge for a couple of days, or freeze in ice cube trays or bags.

\\\ **TIP** ///

For really clear stock, soak the bones for an hour in salted cold water with a tablespoon of white wine vinegar, then rinse.

VEGETABLE STOCK

MAKES 1.25–1.5 litres
PREP TIME: 10 MINS • COOK TIME: 20–25 MINS
WF · GF · DF · V · Ve

Vegetable stock is the simplest and fastest of all the stocks, and involves little skimming, since vegetables won't leach fat into the liquid. This is a white stock, meaning the vegetables are not browned before going into the water, but if you want to make something with a richer, meatier flavour (if you're a vegetarian and you want to use it in place of beef or chicken stock, say), dice and gently brown all the vegetables in a little cooking oil for 10 minutes before adding the water. You will need to skim off any cooking fat that rises to the surface.

2 **onions**, roughly chopped

2 **carrots**, roughly chopped

1 **leek**, trimmed and roughly chopped

2 sticks of **celery**, roughly chopped

2 cloves of **garlic**, halved

2 **bay leaves**

4 sprigs of **fresh thyme**

4 **fresh parsley stalks**

8 **button** or **chestnut mushrooms**

10 whole **black peppercorns**

1–2 litres **water**

Place all the ingredients in a large pan and cover with water – you will need a litre or more. Bring to a gentle simmer, and cook for 15–20 minutes. Strain out the vegetables and discard them, retaining the stock.

Store, covered, in the fridge for a couple of days, or freeze in ice cube trays or ice cube bags.

\\\\ TIP ////

For soups like perky pea and mint (see page 130) or courgette and green herb (see page 38), pea pods briefly simmered along with the other ingredients make a wonderful base.

BONE BROTH

MAKES 1.25–1.5 litres
PREP TIME: 15 MINS · COOK TIME: up to 15 HOURS
WF · GF · DF

1kg **beef bones**, cut into manageable chunks by the butcher (you can also use **chicken** or **pork**, or a mixture)

2 **carrots**, roughly chopped

1 **leek**, trimmed and roughly chopped

1 **onion**, roughly chopped

2 sticks of **celery**

1.5–2 litres **hot water**

2 tablespoons **cider vinegar** or **lemon juice**

½ teaspoon **salt**

This low-and-slow broth is meaty and tasty enough to eat on its own – although it's become very fashionable recently, broth like this has been used across many cultures as a cure-all for hundreds of years.

Heat the oven to 220°C/425°F/gas mark 7. Place the bones in a roasting tin and roast in the oven for 30 minutes, until browned.

Reduce the oven temperature to 100°C/200°F/gas mark ¼. Lift the bones carefully out of the tray, leaving the fat behind (save it for making roast potatoes). Place them in your biggest ovenproof saucepan, with a tight-fitting lid, along with the vegetables. Next, add the hot water. It should cover the bones by at least 3cm, so add more if necessary. Finally, add the vinegar or lemon juice and salt.

Set the pan over a medium heat and bring to a steady boil on the hob. Skim off any scum or foam that forms on the top and discard.

Put a lid on the pan and place it in the low oven. Check back in an hour or so to make sure the liquid is only just bubbling – you are aiming for a very long, very slow cook with hardly any reduction in the water level. If liquid is already disappearing, cut a sheet of baking paper and lay it over the top of the pan, then put the lid on over the paper, to create a tighter seal. Or, if your oven seems to be running too high, turn the temperature down by 10°C/50°F.

Leave in the low oven for at least 12 hours if using beef bones (we cook ours for 15 hours), slightly less for pork, and about 6 hours for chicken.

The broth is ready when the bones are completely stripped of meat and are beginning to disintegrate. Remove from the oven and cool. When you can handle the pan, strain the broth into a jug, using a fine-meshed sieve, and discard the bones and mushy vegetables, keeping the liquid. Place in the fridge to cool completely – the fat will set on top of the broth, making it easy to remove and discard. Drink the broth from a mug when you need some old-fashioned nourishing.

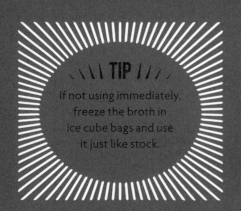

TIP
If not using immediately, freeze the broth in ice cube bags and use it just like stock.

INDEX

ACKNOWLEDGEMENTS

REBECCA: Working with the LEON team on this book has been a real joy. Thank you to John Vincent, who couldn't have made collaborating easier, and everyone in the LEON food team who shared ideas and recipes (especially Rebecca di Mambro), as well as Joelle Davis, who kept the wheels turning and everything on schedule. Rachael Gough and Beth Emmens from LEON's office both gave up precious time to appear in some of the photographs (and got roped into helping out as well); thanks to you both too.

Shooting the book has also been a pleasure, thanks to Steven Joyce's beautiful photography (he may be my husband, but there's no bias here!), food stylist Oliver Rowe, who did a terrific job preparing the food in each picture, and Elayna Rudolphy, who cheerfully and unexpectedly doubled up as a props and food assistant, and was brilliant at both. Through her art direction and design, Jo Ormiston created a fabulous, unique and colourful identity for the book (thanks also to her partner, Saskia, who helped transport the many, many, many bowls we needed...). I would also like to mention the good people at Waters Enterprises, a fishmonger and greengrocer in Forest Hill, South London, who went out of their way to fix us up with good-looking fish and veg, often at short notice.

We're indebted to Ken Yamada and Emma Reynolds, founders of the Tonkotsu group of restaurants. Proper tonkotsu ramen recipes require expert guidance, and they gave us their recipe to publish here. Similarly, thanks to Mandy Yin, director of Sambal Shiok (www.sambalshiok.co.uk), a brilliant Malaysian pop up, for letting us use her laksa recipe; to Meera Sodha for giving us her daily dal recipe, first published in her wonderful cookbook, *Made In India* (Penguin). Food writer, the kindly Uyen Luu (www.uyenluu.com), gave us her amazing vegan pho recipe and Oliver Rowe also donated two recipes – one, a Jerusalem artichoke soup, from his memoir-cookbook, *Food For All Seasons* (Faber), and the other, a beetroot soup with a gingery tofu drizzle, created especially for us. We are really grateful to you all for your generosity and expertise.

Thanks to Alison Starling, Pauline Bache and Jonathan Christie at Octopus Publishing, who made a tight turnaround completely manageable and the whole process calm and achievable. Thanks also to my agent, Antony Topping at Greene and Heaton, for introducing us all.

Finally, thanks to all my neighbours. You ate a lot of experimental soup, and always managed to seem happy about it.

JOHN: Rebecca has acknowledged the people who have been part of this happy soup collective and I would like to sing the soupy praises of Rebecca herself. Talent is one thing, and Rebecca has it: a talent for flavour, fun and finesse. But more than that a partnership needs each partner to care more about the other person than themselves and that has been the case here. I hope we do more together.

My second round of thanks goes to the nearly one thousand people who work at LEON. Our books, our cookware range, our ability to spend time on things like the School Food Plan, are all built on each interaction LEON people have with each guest. Thank you to my LEON colleagues who work long hours with dedication. Thank you to our guests who in total come ten million times a year. We are so grateful for the trust you put in us.

An Hachette UK Company

www.hachette.co.uk

First published in Great Britain in 2017 by
Conran Octopus, a division of
Octopus Publishing Group Ltd
Carmelite House
50 Victoria Embankment
London EC4Y 0DZ
www.octopusbooks.co.uk

ISBN 978-1-84091-759-8

A CIP catalogue record for this book is available from the British Library.

Printed and bound in China

10 9 8 7 6 5 4 3 2 1

PHOTOGRAPHY: Steven Joyce

PUBLISHER: Alison Starling
ART DIRECTION, STYLING & DESIGN: Jo Ormiston
STYLING ASSISTANT: Elayna Rudolphy
FOOD STYLING: Rebecca Seal and Oliver Rowe
CREATIVE DIRECTOR: Jonathan Christie
SENIOR EDITOR: Pauline Bache
COPYEDITOR: Annie Lee
SENIOR PRODUCTION MANAGER: Katherine Hockley

We have endeavoured to be as accurate as possible in all the
preparation and cooking times listed in the recipes in this book.
However they are an estimate based on our own timings during recipe
testing, and should be taken as a guide only, not as the literal truth.
Nutrition advice is not absolute. If you feel you require consultation
with a nutritionist, consult your GP for a recommendation.

Standard level spoon measurements are used in all recipes.

1 tablespoon = one 15 ml spoon
1 teaspoon = one 5 ml spoon

Eggs should be medium unless otherwise stated and preferably
free range and organic. The Department of Health advises that eggs
should not be consumed raw. This book contains dishes made with
raw or lightly cooked eggs. It is prudent for more vulnerable people
such as pregnant and nursing mothers, invalids, the elderly, babies
and young children to avoid uncooked or lightly cooked dishes made
with eggs. Once prepared these dishes should be kept refrigerated
and used promptly.

Fresh herbs should be used unless otherwise stated. If unavailable use
dried herbs as an alternative but halve the quantities stated.

Ovens should be preheated to the specific temperature – if using a
fan-assisted oven, follow manufacturer's instructions for adjusting the
time and the temperature.

This book includes dishes made with nuts and nut derivatives. It is
advisable for customers with known allergic reactions to nuts and
nut derivatives and those who may be potentially vulnerable to these
allergies, such as pregnant and nursing mothers, invalids, the elderly,
babies and children, to avoid dishes made with nuts and nut oils. It is
also prudent to check the labels of pre-prepared ingredients for the
possible inclusion of nut derivatives.

Vegetarians should look for the 'V' symbol on a cheese to ensure it is
made with vegetarian rennet. There are vegetarian forms of Parmesan,
feta, Cheddar, Cheshire, Red Leicester, dolcelatte and many goats'
cheeses, among others.

Not all soy sauce is gluten-free – we use tamari (a gluten-free type of
soy sauce), but check the label if you are unsure.

Remember to check the labels on ingredients to make sure they don't
have hidden refined sugars. Even savoury goods can be artificially
sweetened so it's always best to check the label carefully.

LEON

HAPPY SOUPS

BY REBECCA SEAL & JOHN VINCENT